Selections from
HISTORY TODAY

General Editor
C. M. D. CROWDER

CONFLICTS IN TUDOR AND STUART ENGLAND

A Selection of Articles from *History Today*
with an original introductory essay by

IVAN ROOTS

OLIVER & BOYD
EDINBURGH
LONDON

OLIVER AND BOYD LTD

Tweeddale Court
Edinburgh 1

39A Welbeck Street
London W 1

First published 1967

Printed in Great Britain by
T. & A. Constable Ltd.
Edinburgh

PREFACE

The two centuries that lay between the accession to an English throne of the Welshman, Henry Tudor, and the coming to Great Britain of a German, George of Hanover, are among the most exciting in our history. Many themes may be picked out. Conflict is only one of them, but one as important as it is obvious. Historians have discerned change and tension in religion, in the law and working of the constitution, and in economic life. In society they have discovered, or invented, mobility among the gentry and a crisis of the aristocracy. ("The rise of the middle class", an old favourite, has lately been summarily dismissed as a myth.) For some the developments have amounted to a series of revolutions, quite apart from the two civil wars of the 1640s and the revolution of 1688-9, "glorious" because it never got out of hand. Among the series may be noted the Reformation, the administrative reforms of Thomas Cromwell, a "disassociation of sensibility" in literature, and a scientific revolution in the seventeenth century. There has also been talk of a general, that is, European, crisis. In the interpretation of these difficult matters historians have themselves been sometimes less than urbane. It is difficult to be detached, or to appear disinterested, when approaching a period so full and complicated, in which we can readily trace experiences not unlike those of our own age of disturbance.

History Today has been generous in the attention it has given to this main theme of the era, and the choice of conflicts has not been easy. If those I have settled upon seem at a glance to be mainly political it is not because I would wish to minimise the significance of the kind of social tensions discussed in Professor H. R. Trevor-Roper's "Country House Radicals" (*History Today*, III (1953), pp. 461-8). But a number of such articles has already been reprinted elsewhere and, as even my brief bibliography shows, there are in print collections such as Professor Lawrence Stone's *Social Change and Revolution*. However, none of the topics I have chosen is, in fact, without social and other deep implications. Each of them, even the seemingly trivial London riot of 1517, can be a pointer to sources of conflict in almost every aspect of the life and work of the period. There can be no doubt of the intrinsic interest of the subjects of the articles. But I have also looked for penetration in historical investigation, and for skill and elegance in presentation. Even the most casual reader will, I imagine, agree that I have found them in my six authors.

My thanks are due to Dr C. M. D. Crowder, General Editor of this series, and to Mrs Janet Rae of Oliver and Boyd for their help and encouragement.

IVAN ROOTS

CONTENTS

Ivan Roots

RIOTS AND RISINGS

Conflict is a plangent keynote of the whole Tudor and Stuart era. During these two centuries a nation which today regards itself, somewhat complacently, as well endowed with a sense of order and respect for the rule of law, acquired a reputation for violence and changeability. Englishmen of all classes were then inclined to be noisy and excitable, ever ready with a tear or a blow, intolerant, self-centred, even brutal. They were arrogant, too. For them whatever was English was likely to be good, though they were even more convinced of the superiority of their own "countries", localities like Kent or Yorkshire or the Fens. It is hard to see how a people so little aware of politics, as the art of the possible, and so casual, even in the lip-service which they paid to the virtues of discipline, could ever develop a capacity for compromise. Thomas Hobbes's pessimistic view of the state of man in nature was surely an effect of his experience of the turbulence of his countrymen under the existing forms of government and society.

The passionate Englishman was the product of past and present. Not far behind him was the disorder which

we call "the Wars of the Roses", but which was simply
"the civil wars", until the great catastrophe of the 1640s
usurped that title. The breakdown of the fifteenth
century can be over-stated. It was an age of growth and
construction, too. Yet contempt for the actual operation
of law and insolence towards authority had its chance to
spread, aping the example set by magnates on "parade".
Yorkist and Tudor Kings had to work hard to check it.
They were helped by a reaction among some groups in
favour of more effective control, at any rate of other
people. We can exaggerate the achievement. "Bastard
feudalism", which was not a system but a ragged mani-
festation of anti-social appetites, declined more from the
financial stress of the "good lords" than because plati-
tudinous legislation against livery and maintenance was
suddenly accepted. Throughout the Tudor century
"bully-boys" in the pay of petulant men of substance,
who intended to be dominant either in the nation or in
the local community, disturbed the peace. In 1530, in a
struggle between two rival Newport (Mon.) families, the
Herberts of St Julian's demolished the town bridge to
prevent help coming to the besieged Morgans. This was
private warfare, a revelation of the real standards of the age.

It was a period of acute social and economic strains,
which gave an excuse for unrest, and even incentive to
revolt. Inflation and slumps were, perhaps still are,
mysterious things. Both sovereign and subject were ill-
equipped to cope with them. Poverty, absolute or relative,
led some men to crime, among them a peer like the Earl
of Essex in 1601. Savage penalties by frightened governments might provoke more belligerence than they headed

off. A man would feel that he might as well be hanged for a sheep as for a lamb. Less desperate victims of the maladjusted society could be almost as troublesome, venting their frustration in denunciations of this or that novelty. It was never merry, they said, since monks went down . . . or gentlemen came up . . . or fields were enclosed . . . or whatever. Everybody claimed, inaccurately maybe, but very sincerely, to be sticking to the old known ways. It was always someone else who was innovating and who must be crushed. Stability must be defended, by violence if need be.

Things were never quite as grim as they were reckoned to be: enclosures, for instance, were limited in location and extent. But that there were genuine hardships at all levels is indisputable. It was not in the character of the age to accept this without protest. The literature of complaint is enormous, to say nothing of actual rebellions, which, like the Pilgrimage of Grace, could be really serious. It takes in sermons, preambles to Acts of Parliament, plays, broadsides, poems, treatises, pamphlets, speeches, placards, and proclamations. Students of literature who have so cleverly worked out from Shakespeare and his contemporaries a view of an ordered world, readily accepted as a frame of reference by a diversified audience, should look more closely at a time which was out of joint, certainly not working to rule.

Economic and social tension is not the whole story. Religion, always for some a thing of bread as well as of manna, set men at odds. No doubt the bulk of the nation, considered on the eve of the Reformation rather perfunctorily formal in their observances, continued to

take God for granted under the new dispensations. But
there were those who were deeply stirred. New creeds
and philosophies conspired to put this world and the next
in doubt for some while stiffening the certitudes of
others. In these circumstances it was impossible for a
state, whose pretensions outran its resources, to compel
uniformity, let alone inspire unity. Erratic attempts, by
the post-Reformation state, to realise a claim to control
almost every aspect of national life contributed to an
atmosphere of unease. By 1640 Charles I, heir to Henry
VIII's royal supremacy (that very mixed blessing), was
faced with something like a common opposition among
the political nation. The crisis also gave an opportunity,
partly by accident, partly by the design of devious
politicians, for groups below this level, not always mere
mobs, to express their variable discontents.

Civil war in 1642 was surely not inevitable. It was the
unwelcome outcome of the clash of personalities, and
events, some, like the Ulster Rebellion of 1641, chiefly
external to England. But there were deeper issues and it
is difficult to see how such things could have been
resolved without a show of violence. The Gordian knot
which impatient men could not, for fumbling, untie
would have to be cut. This civil war was waged not only
in the field at Edgehill, but in the press, in St Stephen's
Chapel in Westminster and in the back parlour of the
Swan at Stafford. Violence takes many allotropic forms.
By 1660 most of the political nation, appalled by a
glimpse of anarchy, thought they had had enough. But
few could see a safe way out of the impossible situation.
Return to monarchy, in the old Stuart line, seemed a

desirable end: but it took the enigmatic genius of George Monck, holding off uncontrolled violence by the threat of his own more orderly kind, to bring it about. 1660 was a happy year of restoration of King, Church, and Parliament, of Common Law, and, less remarked at the time, of some of the problems that had brought on the Interregnum. When these problems were joined by new ones a fresh series of heated political and constitutional conflicts was set in motion. Civil war was close at hand in 1679-81 and was certainly to be feared in 1688-9. Somehow or other it was headed off. Yet only after two or three more decades of turbulence would the iron age of the Stuarts make way for the golden stability of the mid-eighteenth century. That did not last long or strike deep. The classical century, the era of Hepplewhite and Chippendale, was also the heyday of veneer.

The articles reprinted in this volume consider six significant episodes, three from the Tudor and three from the Stuart period. Each exposes something of the volatility of the times. Each has some reference to the issues generalised above, though each, it must be said, has its own unique features. Some, like the May Day Riots of 1517 or, perhaps, the Essex Rising of 1601, were comparatively trivial and localised. Others, such as the diversity of opinion in the Long Parliament in 1641 or the Exclusion Crisis, were very serious indeed, sapping at the political, if not the social, order. Behind the verbal excesses lurked physical violence. It is the object of this introduction to examine a few points of contrast and comparison between these diverse conflicts. The reader will be able to make many others for himself.

A prominent thread running through the elaborate tapestry of Tudor and Stuart history is the problem of the succession. It cannot be unravelled without pulling at other threads—religion, foreign policy, prerogative, even trade. All were contentious matters of conflict.

Henry VII assumed the throne in 1485 as the favourite of a god of battles. Possession was nine points of the divine law: but Henry cautiously added a fraction more by marrying Elizabeth of York, a likely rival either by herself or as the tool of a faction. He also got some sort of parliamentary recognition. Even so, he knew his title was weak and felt that he must work hard to head off claimants springing up at home and abroad. His own invasion, the enterprise of a man with no war experience, had been a calculated gamble which had come off. There were other punters: they might be as lucky and even more reckless. So some of Henry's unbounded energies went towards eliminating pretenders, since this was as neces- sary for securing his dynasty as was winning support by acceptable policies. His foreign policy was more dynastic than national. His achievements included a Scottish and— a great *coup*—a Spanish match for his children. Both had unlooked-for consequences.

Henry VIII, with kingship thrust upon him by the death of his brother Arthur, was well aware of the problems of a disputable succession. Life could be short anyway in the sixteenth century and the Tudors were not robust. From the start Henry shot suspicious glances at his relatives. Indeed, he spilled a lot of their royal blood. Ironically his marriage to Arthur's widow, Catherine of Aragon, which he hoped would strengthen his position by a continued alliance with a major European house, proved troublesome. Catherine's failure to produce the obligatory male heir pricked a conveniently, but probably genuinely, queasy conscience. When lust for Anne Boleyn supervened, circumstances came about in which Thomas Cromwell, a singularly clear-sighted politician, could usher in, through Parliament, a Church of England quite independent of the papacy. Henry's tiresome matrimonial ventures did little to ease his situation. Anne Boleyn gave him a daughter, and his son by Jane Seymour, born in October 1537, was a sickly child of nine when called upon to reign. Across his throne fell the shadow of faction, deepened by religious animosities and social unrest. As it became clear that Edward would not live long there was encouragement to interfere with the succession to the crown. So in 1553, John Dudley, Duke of Northumberland, brought forward "the Device", which is the subject of Professor S. T. Bindoff's article.[1] This was a blatant piece of private enterprise owing a lot to the bad example set by Henry VIII's own imperious juggling with the succession.

Much can be said, in fact, for Northumberland's plan. He certainly was factious: but he had a notion of what was likely to be good for the country as well as for himself. He was an able administrator and could argue that his continuance in power would benefit the common weal. An age of tension, even of open revolt, as in Ket's Rising in 1549, called for an experienced, unrelaxing grip. A change in the succession to make permanent the Protector's ascendancy might be both possible and desirable. It

[1] S. T. Bindoff, "A Kingdom at Stake, 1553", pp. 38-52.

might also be acceptable. Mary was an unknown quantity —or rather what was known of her was disturbing. She would obviously try to undo the extended Reformation. Already there was religious strife. An abrupt reversal would intensify it. As it happened envy and hatred of a man who could not fail to make enemies combined with loyalty to the true Tudor line to frustrate what was at best a risky business. Ironically Northumberland ensured the peaceable succession of each in turn of the two women he had worked to exclude.

Mary's reign was brief. The accession of Elizabeth I was eased by the mere fact that her sister had proved, both by practice and by her *Act concerning the Regal Power*, that a woman could rule in England. Mary's inept policies were a help, too. She was misled into imagining that the upsurge of loyalty, which swept her to the throne, meant that her people were inspired with zeal for her religion. She saw herself as God's chosen instrument for releasing England from the sins of her father and brother. The truth is that zealots, Papist or Protestant, were few. Mary's aims needed genuine and extensive enthusiasm, as did James II's a century later. Her attempt to provide it by ceremonial burnings was disastrous. If Mary's days had been longer she might have set off, by reaction, wars of religion akin to those in France, in which there was as much political and social content as religious.

Philip II, for very good reasons, urged moderation. He got no credit for it. Mary's marriage to him was unpopular. It drew gloomy attention to the succession problem. Few Englishmen wanted their island dragged

Henry VIII, after Holbein.

ANNO DNI   · 1 · 5 · 4

LADI MARI   DOVGHTER
THE MOST   VERTVOVS PRI
KINGE HENRI   THE EIGHT

THE AGE OF   XXVIII YER

Queen Mary I, by an unknown artist.

into the expensive international polity of the House of Hapsburg. Some of them were well aware of the centralising tendencies of that gigantic combine. They would resist them both from a national account—England should not dwindle to just another Hapsburg province like Milan or Valencia—and in defence of loyalties at the "grass-roots", since a successful Philip II would expunge local communities within England itself. Besides, it would mean high taxes, as under Wolsey, to pay for wars of no interest to England. Worst of all it would bring in hordes of foreigners competing with Englishmen for jobs and honours. The xenophobia which had flared up in the riots of 1517 was only slumbering. If Philip and Mary had a child (and why should they not?) the future was bleak. Mary proved sterile, but the mere expectation of a pregnancy, joining with other discontents, produced a couple of conspiracies which aimed to alter the succession. They failed but drew attention to genuine problems and made Mary look very warily at her younger sister.

Elizabeth succeeded in 1558. The dangers confronting her may have been exaggerated. There is, for instance, little evidence that anyone worked to impede her accession by force or by a "device". This was fortunate. She reinforced it by prudent, well-advised conduct. She had learned a lot from her sister's errors. No hasty match, Spanish, French, or for that matter, English for her, though the possibility could be made use of. She could not escape all foreign involvement, but she could stop other powers from pulling England about for their own advantage. Inevitably the succession came up for discussion. Mary of Scotland, briefly of France, too,

C.T.S.E.—B

symbolised the danger by quartering the arms of England with her own. Elizabeth was not morbid in seeing Mary as her own likely winding sheet. Her Parliaments expressed fears about the succession as a national interest, which it certainly was. Some members used a brutal frankness of speech which they claimed to be privileged. Her own ministers could not leave the thing alone.

Yet Elizabeth made the "open" succession an instrument, a source of strength. It encouraged hopeful or desperate plots to shorten her reign, which might be brief enough anyway: but it also allowed her to cry up her role as the only screen between a kingdom at peace and one in commotion. It called for skill—she had it. It called for luck—she found that, too. After forty-five years, few of them silent on this topic, she handed over an undisputed throne to the man she had designated, a family man, who would have to find some other argument to back his intention to continue to rule as he imagined Elizabeth had done. (It may be noted that a possible motive in Essex's rebellion lay in the matter of succession. With Elizabeth clearly nearing her end, there was every reason for Essex and his associates to seize power in order to be in a powerful position against all rivals when a new sovereign came in.)

The succession question did not die in 1603, as James's treatment of Arabella Stuart shows. It became acute in 1649. The execution of Charles I was followed by the Rump's repudiation of the Prince of Wales, and the outright abolition of kingship. But the Scots refused to acquiesce. They resented the brash English assumption that they, too, must abandon a Scottish house. Moreover the unfortunate prince might be and, indeed, soon was, persuaded to make big concessions to become King of the Scots and to be helped to restore the throne of England. Dunbar and Worcester defeated that scheme, but Charles miraculously escaped to the Continent, where he was a threat to each successive régime in England. The Rump was harried by the impatient army to provide a respectable successor to itself. Its reluctance "forced" Oliver Cromwell to throw it out. But what to put in its place? The first answer—the Little Parliament, for some the forerunner to the Fifth Monarchy, Christ himself—was a flop. It was followed by a written constitution, the Instrument of Government, which set up "a single person" to head the executive. Oliver Cromwell himself was the only possible candidate for that office —but uncertainty in the succession remained. Who should follow Oliver? Election by a council of state was likely to set off a competition among generals who could try to collect votes on the points of their swords. So in 1657 there came a proposal to make Oliver king.

The Protector was attracted by the offer but after intensive discussion, in which much was said about earlier succession conflicts, rejected it, being pretty sure that the army would not back him. Yet he managed to show that the succession was a vital national concern and won the right to nominate his own successor. Significantly he named his eldest son Richard. Richard's protectorate was a failure largely because of the intractability of his rivals. His sensible resignation left no obvious successor. What happened then is the subject of Professor Austin Wool-rych's article.[2] Charles II soon found, as Mary had done, that enthusiasm for the legitimate succession, brought about in so remarkable a fashion, did not mean that his people were abject and pliable. The violence which had produced the Interregnum was still a feature of political and social life. The reign saw fierce conflicts, crises blown up by faction, religious intolerance, and the opportunism of obstructive politicians mingled with matters of genuine concern to the propertied classes, sometimes even to the whole nation. By the end of the 1670s the issues came to a focus in yet another succession dispute.

Charles II could father illegitimate children but his wife was barren. His heir was his brother, James, Duke of York, considered by many to be "a man for arbitrary power", bad enough, but worse, he was a papist, secretly at first but then openly, even blatantly. The possible accession of this inflexible character, sparked off a struggle, mainly in Parliament, but lunging towards civil war, with mobs out roaming London streets, as they had done in '41, still within living memory. This is described by Professor J. P. Kenyon.[3] The attempt to keep him from the throne was the logical outcome of the policy of excluding Catholics from office. The throne was highest of all political places and still by far the most potent. But the Duke of York's opponents over-reached themselves by their cynical violence and their squabbles about whom or what to put in his stead. Charles stuck

[2] A. H. Woolrych, "The Collapse of the Great Rebellion", pp. 82-101.

[3] J. P. Kenyon, "The Exclusion Crisis", pp. 102-125.

loyally to his brother, who had often exasperated him, and suddenly found himself with a party. So he enjoyed four years of apparent royal triumph before dying in his own bed at Whitehall—a remarkable achievement.

James succeeded peaceably in 1685. Monmouth's bid for the crown collapsed. His execution eased the succession problem not only for James himself but ironically for William of Orange, who in 1688 might have been embarrassed by a live English duke, who was a Protestant, and of royal blood, even if he was a bastard. James misread the signs. He took them to point to acceptance of his policies whatever they might become. Having witnessed the easy loyalty of the Church of England in the crisis years, he presumed it was inexhaustible. It took only three and a half years to prove him wrong. The revolutionary situation at the end of 1688 was the product of a whole concatenation of circumstances, social and political as well as religious, but the succession was probably the catalyst of them all.

In 1685 James's heir was his Protestant daughter Mary, the wife of William of Orange. William was himself a Stuart high on the ladder of succession, and regarded by many as the champion of European protestantism and possible saviour of English protestantism. James was not young and it looked as if any inroads he might make into English religion and liberties, readily equated, would not last long. But in June 1688 Mary of Modena, moved by prayers and pilgrimages, gave birth to a son. Because it was politically desirable that it should be so, it was suggested that the prince was a supposititious child, a comforting belief lightly supported by odd circumstances about the confinement. Genuine or not this child was the heir to the throne, sure to be raised as a Catholic and to give permanence to his father's upsetting policies. It was —or could be made into—a crisis.

William, who had long held a "watching brief" over English affairs—he had, for example, been engrossed in the Exclusion crisis—responded, in the autumn of 1688, to an invitation to intervene. The magnates who asked him said nothing about making him king, but mentioned the falsity of the Prince, reminding William of his wife's and his own rights. It is unlikely that William imagined that he would be able to topple James from the throne without effort: but James, who remembered the story of Richard II, played into his hands by sending the Queen and the Prince out of the country and following them himself soon afterwards. The throne was thereby vacant —though there was a lot of argument about that. If vacant, to be filled by whom? There was really not much choice. William was a man with military power, some political backing and a compliant wife. In February 1689 the open succession was closed by the joint accession of William and Mary. William had sole possession of regal power.

Mary died childless in 1694. William's heir was Mary's staunchly Anglican sister, Anne. But before William died in 1702 the question of succession loomed up again. In 1700 Anne lost her last surviving child, the Duke of Gloucester, at the ripe age of eleven. Preventive measures were called for if the old Stuarts, recognised by Louis XIV, the national enemy, were not to come back. The *Act of Settlement* provided for the succession on Anne's

death of "The Hanoverians", the Protestant descendants
of James I's daughter, Elizabeth of Bohemia. As in 1689
there were to be conditions. These were a scratch lot got
together in response to experience of William III and to
what could be imagined of the newcomers. Some were
rescinded before they actually came over, and the Act
itself did not resolve all difficulties. The worst of these
was Scotland, still a separate kingdom, and likely as in
1649—though not in 1689—to cleave to the elder
branch of the national family. This would be an alarming
circumstance at any time, but it might be disastrous if
Anne died in the middle of a war with France, once
partner with the Scots in the "Auld Alliance". Arguments
for the Union were numerous, so were prejudices against
it. It took patience and a sense of compromise that was
not readily summoned in a reign of bitter faction, such as
Anne's. By 1707 it was achieved; and George of Hanover
came over "in pudding time" in 1714. But the revolts of
'15 and '45 showed that the succession was a matter for
rebellion in the eighteenth century.

The accessions of a Dutchman and a German were
not wildly popular among Englishmen. Reactions to
them expose another thread which runs through many of
the conflicts of this period and which appears in several
of the episodes considered in the articles in this volume.
When one of George I's plump entourage chided an
abusive mob by pointing out that they had come for the
"goods" of the English, some wag promptly added
". . . and our chattels!" The English were usually convinced that they were being exploited by wily foreigners,
not only Continentals, but the Welsh, the Scots, and the

Irish. It was an obsession to be found at all levels of society, especially when there were aliens at the court, as commonly there were. The court was of course the centre of government—and continued to be in spite of the check given to household rule by Thomas Cromwell in the 1530s. It was the prime source of honour, prestige, profit, and opportunity. Its attractions lie at the heart of many of the conflicts touched upon here, of Essex's rising, for instance. Some historians indeed would explain the whole crisis of the seventeenth century—in Europe as in England—in terms of conflicts within, around, about, for and against "the oppressive, corrupt and authoritarian courts" of the era. The presence of favoured foreigners at the English court was an exacerbating factor, which could be sharpened by religious animosities after the Reformation. Popish aliens were more egregious than the Protestant sort. Popery was not only anti-Christ, but rapidly became unEnglish. Oliver Cromwell characterised papists as "Spaniolised".

Aliens not only endangered English religion while lapping up the cream of the court. They were also involved in industry and trade, internal and external. The fact that without them many enterprises would never have got off the ground was an offence in itself. A self-centred people, the English saw arrogance sustained by roguery and rapacity in alien advancement. Niggling resentment could turn into violence—as it did in May 1517, an episode described by Mr Martin Holmes.[4] This abrupt affair draws attention, too, to other aspects of

[4] Martin Holmes, "Evil May Day 1517: the Story of a Riot", pp. 22-37.

Tudor conflicts: the lack of state resources for the maintenance of public order, the importance of London and the possibilities of the pulpit for propaganda are a few of these.

Northumberland's "device" has a hint of xenophobia. Mary was a "Spanish Tudor"—Lady Jane Grey was English. As we have seen Northumberland's failure left England exposed to European encroachment, through Mary's marriage, an affront to her insularity. There is evidence that under Mary Spaniards were reviled. She had to issue edicts about it. They seem to have been implemented no more readily than any other unwelcome legislation in this period. Elizabeth I made her "mere Englishness" a part of her charm and was able to blow her people's local patriotism into something like jingoism. She drifted into war with Spain, but if Spaniards were in general kept out—there were in fact some Spanish refugees living in England—other aliens flocked over— from France, the Netherlands, some even, like Sir Horatio Palavicino, from as far afield as Italy. As usual they strengthened the economy, but remained sources of conflict which flared up when times were bad.

James I not only came from Scotland, he brought Scots to court, and worked to unite in himself two nations as well as two crowns. He failed to dissolve the hard core of mutual suspicions. His son, by trying to bring Scotland into line with England, a policy character- istic of the centralising trend of the times, in fact drove his opponents, in both kingdoms, into a brotherly associa- tion which helped to bring on the civil war and to keep it going. But basic incompatibilities survived and the allies fell out, as brethren will. In 1649 and on many later occasions enmity came into the open. Not until the reign of Anne was a genuine Union conceivable. Even then, as we have seen, it was hard work to get it and long afterwards anti-Scots feelings were expressed, as in the pungent comments of Samuel Johnson.

The Irish were even more disliked in the seventeenth century, being regarded as culturally inferior and tarnished by their Popery. Essex might blame Irish rebels for keeping him too long away from the seats of power in England. The hair-raising tales of bloody massacre in the rising of 1641 helped to inflame the opinions which divided the Long Parliament, and which are discussed in the article by Mr D. H. Pennington.[5] Oliver Cromwell's savage suppression of Ireland was not regarded with so much as distaste by many of his contemporaries and his settlement was not undone at the Restoration. Fears of Irish regiments brought over to reduce England helped to ruin Strafford in 1641, to vilify the royal cause in the civil war and to undermine James II. The setting-up of a provisional government in December 1688 was partly justified by mob excesses on "Irish Night", when wild rumours of the approach of Irish troops swept the capital. It is significant that the Dutch troops of William of Orange, who were cheered as deliverers when they first entered London, were a few weeks later reviled, a circumstance which prompted Sir John Reresby to reflect on the strange mutability of the English people. William

[5] D. H. Pennington, "A Day in the Life of the Long Parliament", pp. 65-81.

III as a Dutchman liked Dutchmen and was himself disliked for it. There are terms in the *Act of Settlement* which amount to an unkind comment on his generosity to his compatriots. The Hanoverians were expected to do the same by their German favourites. It would be pleasant to record that by the end of this period English xenophobia was receding. There are a few hints that it was, in the treatment of Huguenot refugees for example: but the general impression remains that little advance towards tolerating strangers had been made. In the twentieth century experience of England could still make an intelligent and kindly-disposed Dutchman enquire "The English, are they human?"

Each of the conflicts examined in this volume can be discussed in the light of important, even fundamental, social and political issues. Yet each one is also signed by the personalities of individuals. An egocentric age, while it talked, often with eloquence, about splendid ideals of communal harmony gave opportunities, eagerly exploited, for individual ambitions. Bacon's essays on "Ambition" and "Great Place" are not literary exercises but the heart-felt expression of a man who had flung himself into the experience of his times.

It was the personal grievances of John Lincoln, the talkative broker, that helped to bring about the Riot of 1517. In its suppression we can discern a conflict between the ambitions of Cardinal Wolsey and the Howard clan, who are found hovering around the centres of faction throughout the whole period. (Faction was widely deplored, but somehow or other nearly always prospered.) Northumberland's concern for himself and his family is

patent, and the failure of the "Device" came as much
from the contrary ambitions of flexible politicians as
from the glamour of the main Tudor line in the drab
person of Mary I. Essex's rising, as Mr Penry Williams[6]
shows, was much more a gesture of frustration by a
greedy, rather naïve, climber than the last fling of a dying
feudalism. Essex had been edged out into the cold. He
saw his distress as the direct result of the machinations of
the Cecils. So with the high-spirited gentlemen of broken
fortunes who followed or pushed him on, he lashed out,
putting the state in jeopardy for personal ends. In this
way the crisis of the aristocracy could become the crisis
of the realm. Essex's rising seems complex enough: there
are those puritan preachers to be accounted for. But
it is doubtful if protestantism really exercised a shallow
mind obsessed by prestige and profit.

The debates of November 1641, of which Mr Pennington has selected one important but not exceptional day,
had rather more content. The initial seeming unanimity
of the Long Parliament was crumbling. Arguments
revealed deep-seated differences on major national issues.
Nonetheless personalities and private interests ran
through all the proceedings of this Parliament, from the
King downwards. Sir Edward Dering was a fussy
opinionated man who printed his speeches to please and
justify himself. John Pym himself was no more "a
principle" than was Richelieu. He was an individual
of remarkable complexity, whose actions can be partly
explained by a desire to excel and to survive. The civil
war that followed less than a year after this hard day's

6 Penry Williams, "The Fall of Essex", pp. 53-64.

debating expressed the hopes and failures of ambitious men. To suggest that Edward Hyde turned to Charles I out of pique at Pym's ascendency would be grossly unfair, but it would be foolish to ignore a hint of personal rivalry.

The fall of the English republic, as Professor Woolrych shows, owed a good deal to personalities. Certainly between 1658 and 1660 there were genuine arguments over principles but the protagonists simply could not sink their personal differences. Their ambitions enabled Monck to realise a private desire, shared with his formidable wife, to become the saviour of society. Two decades later the Exclusion crisis gave full play to self-seeking politicians, some left over from the Interregnum. This is not the whole story, though it is fashionable to seek to rob the reign of Charles II of all contact with principles. Even Shaftesbury, "false Achitophel", had to have something more than prejudices and opportunism to work on.

There are many other sources of conflict touched upon in these articles, which themselves consider only a few turbid occasions. The careful reader may find himself reacting against what must seem the directing notion of this introduction—the desire to establish willy-nilly something common to all these disparate *coups*, plots, arguments, and crises. He may feel that each has its unique qualities. He will be right. It is a salutary exercise to attempt to find them. But it is one without an end.

Martin Holmes

EVIL MAY-DAY 1517:
the Story of a Riot [1]

It is no unfamiliar thing for friction to arise between the
native Englishman and the settler from overseas. For a
long time denizen and alien will live together and work
together in neighbourly fashion, with a degree of
friendliness and mutual respect, and then some intrusive
factor will set them at each other's throats, arousing hard
feelings and even bloodshed, till the disturbance has to
be quelled by authority and all becomes quiet again until
the next time.

One such event, which occurred nearly four and a half
centuries ago, is worthy of note because it is unusually
well recorded by the leading historians of the day, who
give us not only an account of the disturbance but an
insight into the motives and personalities of some of the
people concerned. Edward Hall, the chronicler, and
Richard Grafton, Hall's publisher and a chronicler in his
own right, were of an age to have heard first-hand
accounts of the May-Day riots of 1517; while John Stow,

[1] [Copyright © Martin Holmes. Originally published in *History
Today*, XV (1965), pp. 642-50.]

whose great work of research into London history and topography began only after Hall's death, knew Grafton well enough to quarrel with him and engage in a paper warfare of treatise and counter-treatise, each loftily impugning the other's accuracy and scholarship and occasionally descending to childish puns upon the other's name. Still, the narratives of all are valuable; and we shall see how, by collating one with another, we find the whole story taking coherent shape.

It began, Hall and Grafton tell us, with an unfortunate coincidence of anti-alien tension on several levels at once. The court of the young and wealthy Henry VIII was full of continental financiers—Frenchmen, Lombards, and Genoese—engaged in negotiating loans abroad, notably a loan of thirty thousand pounds to the Emperor Maximilian. One of the principal agents in this transaction went bankrupt and the other absconded, so Maximilian never got his loan and Henry never got his money back; and a good many English merchants were ruined through having supplied goods on credit to the foreigners. Before this crash, however, the "strangers" had matters all their own way and "boasted themselves to be in such favour with the King and his Council that they set naught by the rulers of the City". For instance, a Lombard called Francesco de' Bardi prevailed on a London merchant's wife to come to his lodging and bring her husband's plate with her. The merchant demanded first his wife and then his plate, tried to bring an action in Guildhall, and was outfaced so boldly that he lost his case and became a laughing-stock. Foreign merchants brought in continental silks, wine, metalwork, and the like, and bought up

English merchandise to re-sell it more profitably abroad; so that the English manufacturer and the English exporter had little chance of keeping themselves in business. The very markets went short of commodities, because the various foreign colonies on the outskirts of London were able to "forestall" or intercept the normal market-produce on its way in, and acquire the best of it before it got to the ordinary citizen. The merchant, the courtier, the artisan, and the London housewife all found themselves complaining of the arrogance and rapacity of aliens who, by virtue of their wealth, court-influence, diplomatic privilege or sheer weight of numbers, bade fair to carry all before them.

Matters came to a head in the spring of 1517. Stow, in his *Survey of London*, gives the date as Palm Sunday, 5 April, when a broker named John Lincoln took steps to bring the scandal to public notice. Before the institution of the popular press, the man who had a grievance was obliged either to print and distribute a pamphlet about it, or to address a meeting, if he could call one together, and express his indignation. Publication cost money; distribution had its difficulties; and it was better to address an audience, or get someone else to explain one's own grievance to an audience convened for some other purpose. And London in the springtime provided an unexampled opportunity in the shape of the Easter sermons.

Rhetoric was an important subject in the sixteenth-century schoolboy's curriculum. It had its fine points of technique, both in the marshalling of arguments and in their actual delivery to a listening public; and a Tudor

Edward VI, School of Holbein.

National Portrait Gallery

Elizabeth I, by an unknown artist.

audience was swift to consider both the matter and the manner of a discourse. Attendance at open-air sermons, when days were no longer dark and cold, was a pleasurable exercise, which combined edification with emotional excitement and intellectual entertainment. Shakespeare's Romans, commenting on the oratory of Brutus and of Antony, give a reasonable picture of an audience enthusiastic rather than intelligent, while the great speech of the Archbishop of Canterbury, at the council-board of Henry V, conforms to the orthodox rules of rhetoric, starting with a clear setting-forth of the argument, continuing with emotional exhortation and summing-up by drawing a parallel with some part of the organised processes of nature—in this case, the habits and discipline of the bees. Audiences liked listening to good oratory, whether it was in the theatre, in the law-courts or at a church service; and there were special arrangements at Easter for a series of sermons at the two great open-air pulpits of St Paul's and St Mary Spital.

Paul's Cross, as it was called, is familiar from more than one illustration, and its site on the north side of the cathedral is marked by a modern monument. Less well known today is the preaching-cross outside the Hospital of St Mary Without Bishopsgate. The Hospital was a house of regular canons, and went the way of many other such establishments at the time of the Dissolution of the Monasteries: but its churchyard pulpit-cross, and the custom of its Easter sermon, lasted well on into the seventeenth century. Stow says:

> Time out of mind it hath been a laudable custom that on Good Friday in the afternoon some especial learned

man, by appointment of the Prelates, hath preached a sermon at Paul's Cross treating of Christ's Passion, and upon the three next Easter holidays, Monday, Tuesday and Wednesday, the like learned men, by the like appointment, have used to preach on the forenoons at the said Spital, to persuade the Article of Christ's Resurrection, and then on Low Sunday one other learned man at St. Paul's Cross to make rehearsal of those former sermons, either commending or reproving them as to him (by judgment of the learned divines) was thought convenient. And that done, he was to make a sermon of his own study, which in all were five sermons in one.

The whole programme, in fact, comprised a short course of Easter lectures, with a commentary and concluding summary, and would be welcome to many as a guide to their own private contemplation. The Mayor and Aldermen attended the Good Friday sermon in their violet mourning-gowns, the Monday and Tuesday Spital sermons in scarlet, the Wednesday sermon in violet again, re-appearing in scarlet on Low Sunday for the concluding "exercise" at Paul's Cross. Altogether, the occasion was a formal and solemn one, and the preacher on any of the days concerned could be sure of a large and distinguished audience, including the First Citizen of London himself. It showed a certain audacity, therefore, in John Lincoln to approach the Easter Monday preacher a week beforehand, rehearse his indictment of foreigners in general, and the hardship caused to Londoners by their conduct, and ask the preacher, a Doctor Standish, to make a point of it in his sermon; and it is not surprising that Standish declined to do anything of the sort.

Lincoln's reaction to this rebuff was to take his grievance
to Doctor Bell, a canon of the Spital, who was appointed
to preach on the Tuesday. Doctor Bell heard him out,
agreed that, if matters really were as Lincoln had represented, the case was a serious one, and finally undertook
to "do for the reformation of this matter as much as a
priest may do". Lincoln supplied him with a long
memorandum, setting out the iniquities of the aliens, and
he went away to study it; while Lincoln, who seems from
Hall's narrative to have been something of a busybody
and a thoroughly indiscreet one at that, "went from man
to man saying that shortly they should hear news, and
daily excited young people and artificers to bear malice
to the strangers".

Tuesday came; and, before beginning his discourse,
the preacher announced that a pitiful state of things had
been brought to his notice, and read out the opening of
Lincoln's memorandum. Hall gives the text of it, showing
that it complained how "the aliens and strangers eat the
bread from the poor fatherless children, and take the
living from all the artificers, and the intercourse from all
merchants, whereby poverty is so much increased that
every man bewaileth the misery of other, for craftsmen
be brought to beggary and merchants to neediness". This
was inflammatory enough: but Lincoln proceeded to urge
all citizens to unite "and not to suffer the said aliens so
highly in their wealth". At about this point, the preacher
stopped reading the memorandum, gave out his own
text, "The heaven of heavens is the Lord's, but the earth
hath he given to the children of men", and roundly
declared it the duty of Englishmen to "defend themselves

and to hurt and grieve aliens for the common weale". The sermon was naturally encouraging to the indiscreet, and caused a certain amount of xenophobic talk in the course of the week. On the Sunday following, the Court was at Greenwich and the foreign merchants were very much in evidence, including that Francesco de' Bardi who had made so free with a citizen's wife and plate. They treated the matter as a great jest, laughing and declaring that they would do as much to the Mayor if they got the chance. Sir Thomas Palmer bluntly told them that they enjoyed too much favour in England; and a mercer named William Bolt said to the Lombards "By the Mass, we will one day have a day at you, come when it will". This remark in its turn was remembered and passed round among the citizens, "and the young and evil-disposed people said they would be revenged on the merchants strangers as well as the artificers strangers".

The Court moved to Richmond next day, but left the rumours stirring in the City for another ten days or so, and certain people began to be apprehensive with the approach of May Morning, which was the next occasion for miscellaneous London festivity. Stow has recorded for us how, on that morning, all who could do so would "walk into the sweet meadows and green woods, there to rejoice their spirits with the beauty and savour of sweet flowers and with the harmony of birds praising God in their kind". The fresh countryside came very close to the walls of the City, and it was no long journey for the Londoner to go Maying in the greenwood. Only two years before, King Henry and his Queen had ridden from Greenwich to Shooter's Hill on May Day, in the morning,

to be saluted by a company of bowmen under a leader
who called himself Robin Hood and entertained the royal
party with a display of archery and a meal of venison and
wine, served to them in arbours made from boughs and
ornamented with flowers; and similar pageants and
breakfast parties, on a smaller scale, might be held by
guilds, fraternities, and individual citizens. Young girls
would go out to bathe their faces in hawthorn-dew,
gathered on May Morning, as a charm to preserve their
beauty, while young and old of both sexes would bring
home green boughs and flowers to adorn the house-
fronts. Boys would fence with sword and buckler, and
girls dance for garlands hung across the streets, as was
done at Midsummer; and puritanical writers like Stubbes
maintained that many people went out for no good
purpose, and came home none the better for it.

Spirits ran high, as was natural, in the days before the
festival; and on 28 April there were isolated assaults on
foreigners in the streets, some being cuffed and beaten
and some thrown down into the "channel" or central
gutter. The City authorities took action, and various
culprits, including a skinner named Studley and two men
named Betts and Stephenson, were promptly arrested and
sent to jail, some to Newgate and some to the different
"Counters" or minor houses of detention. It was after
that that a rumour began to go round that on May Day
there would be a comprehensive massacre of aliens by
the Londoners. No one could say where the tale had
started: but it was passed from mouth to mouth and
created a reasonable apprehension among the foreign
residents, some of whom left the City in alarm. It even

reached the Court; and that, perhaps, was where the trouble began.

We have seen in our own day how a comparatively small incident can be magnified out of all proportion—by a newspaper article, perhaps, or a radio or television broadcast—until it is widely rumoured, on no particular authority, that there will be trouble on the next Bank Holiday, and there are arguments—usually among those least informed and least concerned—about the measures that should be taken to control the disturbance when it comes. Things appear to have taken very much the same course in 1517: the prompt action of the authorities was followed by well-meaning, but rather heavy-handed, intervention from Whitehall.

It was not yet called Whitehall, of course. It was still known as York Place, the palace of the King's Chancellor, Thomas Wolsey, Archbishop of York and lately created Cardinal. To the ordinary Londoner he seemed as rich as the King, quite as powerful and even more terrible. Henry, after all, was only twenty-six, and associated in men's minds with sport, May games, pageantry, and the hunting-field: but the Cardinal was the figure that domi- nated the council-board, striking it with his rod when he was moved to anger, and bullying and browbeating any who dared to contradict him. John Skelton has left us an expressive word-picture of Wolsey in *Why Come ye not to Court?* And, even allowing for prejudice and exaggera- tion, there is still a significant correspondence between the poet's roaring Cardinal and the stern Chancellor described by the contemporary historian.

Hall himself was then at Cambridge: but he had ample

opportunity to hear the scene described, later on, by people who had taken part in it, and we may therefore accept his account of the conversation as fundamentally accurate. His own narrative runs briefly but expressively thus:

> This bruit came so far that it came to the King's council, insomuch as the Cardinal, being Lord Chancellor, sent for John Rest, Mayor of the city, and others of the council of the city and demanded of the Mayor in what case the city stood, to whom he answered that it was well and in good quiet. "Nay", said the Cardinal, "it is informed us that your young and riotous people will rise and distress the strangers; hear ye of no such thing?" "No, surely," said the Mayor, "and I trust so to govern them that the King's peace shall be observed, and that I dare undertake if I and my brethren and aldermen may be suffered". "Well", said the Cardinal, "go home and wisely pursue this matter, for if any such thing be, you may shortly prevent it".

There is an ominous sound about that last remark; and the Mayor can have had no illusions about where the blame would fall if anything went wrong. He called a hasty meeting at Guildhall; but it had been four o'clock in the afternoon when he and his companions left York Place, and the whole council could not be assembled until nearly seven. The Recorder, Richard Brooke, reported that the King's Council had heard rumours of an intended rising; the aldermen answered that they had heard the rumour but did not take it too seriously, adding the face-saving rider that "it was well done to foresee it". The Recorder proposed the setting up of "a substantial watch . . . of honest persons, householders, which might withstand the evil-doers": but an alderman objected that it was a bad thing to put men under arms, as no one could be sure which side they would take if there should be trouble. Yet another alderman moved: "that it were best to keep the young men asunder, and every man to shut his doors and to keep his servants within". The Recorder took these various opinions to Wolsey before eight, and came back at half-past, accompanied by Sir Thomas More, recently appointed Under-Sheriff of London, with the Council's instructions that there was to be no armed watch, but that every citizen was to keep himself and his servants indoors until seven o'clock on May Morning.

It was rather late in the day to announce a nine o'clock curfew and expect the announcement to be heard, reported and instantly obeyed: but Sir John Munday, one of the aldermen, seems to have been less than tactful when, on his way back from his ward, he found a crowd of young men in Cheapside watching two of their fellows at the traditional sword-and-buckler play. He told them to stop; and, when one young man asked him why, he replied: "Thou shalt know", and took him by the arm in summary arrest. To a May Eve crowd that had heard nothing of the emergency regulations, this would seem a flat breach of traditional privilege, and was met in the traditional way. The cry went up for "Prentices!" and "Clubs!"; the young man was firmly removed from the alderman's grasp; cudgels and weapons were fetched out from the houses, and the alderman had to take to his heels. Once again Hall's description is as good as any:

> Then more people arose out of every quarter, and out came Servingmen, and Watermen, and Courtiers, and

by a XI of the clock there were in Chepe six or seven
hundred. And out of Paul's Churchyard came three
hundred which wist not of the other, and so out of all
places they gathered, and brake up the Counters, and
took out the prisoners that the Mayor had thither committed for hurting of the strangers, and came to Newgate
and took out Studley and Petyt, committed thither for
that cause.

The original affray had now become a matter of jail-
breaking; and the crowd of resentful apprentices and
watermen was enlarged by a number of men who had
been arrested already for acts of violence. The Mayor and
Sheriffs "made proclamation in the King's name, but
nothing was obeyed", and the whole band ran through
St Nicholas' Shambles to St Martin's-le-Grand, where
they were met by Sir Thomas More, who tried to persuade them to disperse and go home.

Unfortunately, some of the residents in St Martin's
"threw out stones and bats and hurt divers honest persons
that were persuading the riotous people to cease"; and,
though the law-abiding citizens called to them to stop,
they went on throwing brickbats and hot water with more
enthusiasm than accuracy, and Nicholas Downes, one of
the sergeants-at-arms, was badly hurt. He lost his temper
and cried "Down with them"; the mob broke into the
houses, smashed the furniture and threw it out of the
windows, and then swept along Cheapside and Cornhill
to a house near Leadenhall called the Green Gate, the
dwelling of John Meautys, an influential merchant from
Picardy, and French secretary to the King. He was
notoriously unpopular, as the patron of Frenchmen in

general and illicit wool-carders in particular; and it was
just as well that he was not to be found. At which, the
mob fell to looting and then went on to wreck some
foreign shoemakers' premises in Fenchurch Street.

Meanwhile, Sir Thomas Parr went to Whitehall and
gave the alarm to the Cardinal, and on to Richmond to
tell the King. Henry seems to have suspected Parr of
exaggeration; he sent independently to London for news,
and learned that the riot was already over and the ring-
leaders under arrest. Wolsey had fortified his house, and
the Lieutenant of the Tower had shown his dislike of the
city by bombarding it with ordnance: but, at about three
in the morning, the commotion died down of its own
accord, and the authorities had arrested three hundred of
the rioters on their way home. Two hours later, the Earls
of Shrewsbury and Surrey arrived, with such powers as
they could raise: but by that time everything was over.

The trouble was traced back to Dr Bell's Easter
sermon. He and Lincoln were arrested and sent to the
Tower; and on Monday 4 May, the prisoners were
brought through the streets—men, youths, and boys in
their teens—to appear before a court consisting of the
Mayor, the Earl of Surrey, and his father the old Duke of
Norfolk, who was supposed to bear the citizens a grudge
over the death of a dissolute chaplain of his in Cheapside.
The charge, to the consternation of many, was not riot
but High Treason, on the ground that, since the King was
at peace with all Christian princes, any deliberate assault
on aliens was a breach of truce and might be taken as an
act of war. Ten or eleven pairs of gallows were made,
mounted on wheels so that they could be moved easily

about the streets; and thirteen of the rioters were condemned and "executed in most rigorous manner, for the
Lord Edmund Howard, son to the Duke of Norfolk and
Knight Marshal, showed no mercy but extreme cruelty
to the poor younglings in their execution". The words
of the chronicler suggest that the young men suffered
the extreme penalty for High Treason—half-hanging,
mutilation and disembowelling while still alive, and
subsequent hacking into quarters—and this may explain
the events of the following Thursday, when Lincoln and
another group of rioters were led out to die. Lincoln, as
unquestionably the originator of the whole trouble, was
put to death first; and, when the others had the ropes
ready about their necks, orders came from the young
King to hold over the executions. The prisoners were
taken back to gaol, the armed troops of the Howards were
withdrawn from London; and the remaining trials were
deferred to an unspecified date.

Howes, in his edition of Stow's *Annals*, and Godwin,
in his history of the reigns of Henry VIII, Edward VI,
and Mary, relate that this sudden clemency arose from
the intercession of three kneeling Queens—the King's
own consort, Catherine of Aragon, and his sisters the
Queens of Scotland and of France—supported by the
advice of Wolsey: but the episode is not mentioned by
Hall or Grafton, nor is it to be found in the 1592 edition
of the *Annals*, published under Stow's own supervision.
When Howes and Godwin wrote, there was a Stuart on
the throne; and it would be natural to include an anecdote,
historical or not, that did credit to Margaret of Scotland,
the ancestress through whom the house of Stuart had

inherited England's crown. She was certainly in London at the time, staying at Baynard's Castle by Blackfriars when she was not at Court, and returned to her own country in the third week in May. The triple intercession may have taken place as related: but in any event, on Monday 11 May, the King went from Richmond to his Manor of Greenwich, where the Recorder and certain aldermen waited upon him, in black gowns, and begged him on their knees to pardon their own negligence and show mercy to the offenders. He rated them soundly and told them to apply to Wolsey, who would let them know his master's pleasure.

Hall and Grafton say that Queen Margaret left London for Scotland on 18 May, and that the last episode of the treason trials took place on Thursday the 22nd: but Stow puts it as early as the 13th. Similarly, he gives the number of gibbets as ten, as opposed to the earlier writers' eleven. One would be tempted to accept Hall and Grafton as right, were it not that 22 May in that year was a Friday.

Whatever the day, there was a great assembly in Westminster Hall. The King himself sat under a cloth of estate at the upper end, occupying the judgment-seat still commemorated in the name of the King's Bench. With him were the Cardinal, as Chancellor, the Dukes of Norfolk and Suffolk, the Earls of Shrewsbury and Surrey and many other lords and councillors. The Mayor and aldermen, and other City officers, were in attendance by nine in the morning, in their best gowns and suitably briefed by Wolsey; and at the King's command the prisoners were brought in, four hundred men and eleven women, in their shirts and with ropes about their necks

as if prepared for instant execution. The Cardinal roundly
taxed the Mayor and aldermen with negligence; and the
prisoners were told that they "had deserved death for
their offence. Then all the prisoners together cried
'Mercy, gracious lord, mercy'. Then the lords altogether
besought his Grace of mercy, at whose request the King
pardoned them all."

Hall's wording is a little ambiguous here. The words
"his Grace" may refer to the Cardinal or to the King;
and in the latter event, "whose" refers to the suppliant
lords, though it is clear that Wolsey was doing his best
to take charge of the whole ceremony. The popular voice,
however, acclaimed the King. The prisoners plucked the
halters from their necks and flung them into the air as
they cheered; and certain opportunists, including the
man who had actually started the looting but had evaded
arrest, got themselves included in the general pardon by
hastily pulling off their doublets and tossing up ropes
which they had providently brought with them in
anticipation of some such climax.

The matter passed off accordingly with a reprimand
for the City authorities, great publicity for Wolsey, and
increased popularity for the King. Yet, on reflexion, it
seems to have been the City authorities who really put
down the riot. The Howards were very zealous over the
executions, until the King stopped them, and Wolsey
himself, with his sudden alarm and insistence on emergency precautions at the last minute, cannot escape
responsibility for having precipitated the whole affair.

S. T. Bindoff

A KINGDOM AT STAKE 1553 [1]

Henry VIII's persistent quest of heirs, which did so much to shape his reign, had, by its close, yielded him three. They were his son Edward, a boy of nine, and his two daughters, Mary, aged thirty-two, and Elizabeth, aged fourteen. After them came the collateral heirs, the descendants of Henry's two sisters. The elder sister, Margaret, was represented by her daughter, Margaret Countess of Lennox, and by two grandchildren, Mary Queen of Scots, and Henry Lord Darnley (the cousin whom Mary was in due course to marry); the younger one, Mary, by her daughter Frances Duchess of Suffolk, and that lady's daughters, the three Grey sisters, and (through a younger daughter already deceased) the Lady Margaret Clifford.

It is a fact at once remarkable and pertinent that, after Prince Edward himself, all but one of the potential claimants were women. (The single exception, Lord Darnley, could scarcely be regarded as a serious competitor.) This preponderance of females would have been

[1] [Copyright © S. T. Bindoff. Originally published in *History Today*, III (1953), pp. 642-8.]

enough in itself to confuse the succession. But a situation already difficult was further complicated by the fact that the order of succession had been altered more than once during Henry's reign to fit the changing marital fortunes of the king. Thus the Princesses Mary and Elizabeth had each in turn been declared illegitimate and incapable of succeeding. These changes had themselves encouraged the idea that the succession to the throne was not something settled and unalterable, but that it could, and perhaps should, be regulated by the reigning sovereign in what he considered the national interest.

So it came about that, when Henry died in 1547, the succession was governed by the provisions set forth in two documents. The first of these documents was an Act of Parliament. Passed in 1544, that Act declared the

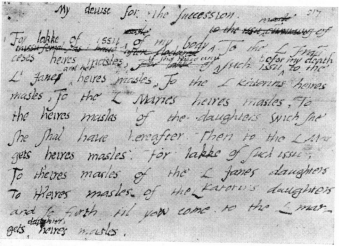

"The Device" by Edward VI, showing the alteration from "L' Janes heires masles", to "L' Jane and her heires masles".

succession to be vested in Edward, Mary, and Elizabeth, in that order. But the right of the two princesses to succeed was at the same time made dependent upon such conditions as the King himself should prescribe, either in his will or in letters patent. By another clause of the Act any attempt to obstruct its implementation was declared to be treason. The second document was Henry VIII's will. This confirmed the order of succession laid down in the Act, but extended it to include the three Grey sisters, in order of seniority, and after them Margaret Clifford. Of the conditions forecast in the Act, the will contained but one, namely, that if either Mary or Elizabeth should marry without the consent of the Privy Council she should forfeit her place in the line of succession. This obvious safeguard against an attempt by any scheming nobleman to secure the substance of kingship, if not the crown itself, by marrying one of these two princesses was to add, as we shall see, another element to the problem.

Edward VI succeeded his father in 1547 without trouble or dispute. But his brief reign went far towards ensuring that the next succession would be a contested one. To begin with, Edward was a minor, and the vacuum which his infancy created in the headship of the state had to be filled, in the absence of princes of the blood, by men who were not of royal birth. Two leading noblemen, Edward Seymour, Duke of Somerset, and John Dudley, Duke of Northumberland, seized the opportunity to play successively the role of Regent or Protector, that is, of king in all but name: and it was the power which Northumberland thus acquired that he attempted to prolong by tampering with the succession to the boy King. For Edward was not only a boy: he was a sickly boy. Had he enjoyed normal health, his minority, and with it the necessity of a Regent, would have had a foreseeable limit. Edward would have become eighteen, the usual age of royal majority, in October 1555: and what we know of him suggests that he would then have taken over the direction of affairs and have managed them as personally and as purposefully as his father and grandfather had done. But from early in his reign it became doubtful whether he would live so long, and the problem of the succession acquired an urgency which only increased with the deterioration in the King's health. As we shall see, it was the fluctuating prospect of Edward's survival which set the tempo of Northumberland's scheming.

As Protector in fact, if not in name, of the young King from the end of 1549, when he overthrew Somerset, Northumberland attained a position in the State which he could not hope to retain under a less complaisant successor. But according to the Henrician settlement Edward's successor was to be the Princess Mary: and from Northumberland's standpoint the succession of Mary would be fatal. That this was so was, of course, largely a matter of religion. Under Northumberland, the country took a further long step—marked by the Prayer Book of 1552—towards Protestantism, and it was only in an England which remained Protestant that he could hope to keep power. But the advancing Protestantism of the reign had no more intrepid or resolute opponent than the Princess Mary herself. Daughter of the Queen whose divorce had heralded the English Reformation, Mary had never wavered in her hostility to that great change of religious allegiance and policy, and it could not be doubted that her accession would mean some—although how much none could foretell—putting back of the clock: it would certainly involve the downfall of those who had identified themselves with the Protestant cause, and among them none more certainly than Northumberland himself.

This, then, was the situation, itself a product of political and religious conflict, which produced Northumberland's conspiracy to alter the succession. In considering that conspiracy, we must begin by noticing that there was no real chance of the Duke's prolonging his supremacy beyond Edward's lifetime, within the framework of Henry's settlement. The only possibility of that kind, a marriage with either Mary or Elizabeth, was practically ruled out by the requirement that it should have the consent of the Privy Council. True, this did not prevent Northumberland—like Somerset's ambitious brother Thomas Seymour before him—from at least contemplating this way out of his difficulty. But, in the upshot, nothing came of these imaginings.

For Northumberland, then, there was no way of escaping ruin save by altering the succession as regulated by Henry VIII. To bring this about legally, or at least legalistically, two things were necessary: the Act of 1544 must be repealed, and Henry VIII's will must be set aside. The first of these would require the co-operation of Parliament, the second could be effected with the consent of the King and Council. Let us try to reconstruct the development of Northumberland's plot to achieve either or both of these objects.

The tempo and chronology of the plot were, as has already been suggested, dictated by the changes in Edward's health. The King's last and fatal illness was preceded by two others, each of which in turn marked a stage in the evolution of Northumberland's plan. The first, an obscure but grave illness, occurred in November 1550. It coincided with a rumour, the first of its kind, that Northumberland was going to marry the Princess Elizabeth. (As we have seen, such a marriage represented the only possibility, albeit a remote one, of Northumberland's attaining his objective within the terms of Henry's settlement, and it may thus be regarded as the first and simplest form of the plot.) Eighteen months later, in April 1552, Edward was attacked simultaneously by measles and smallpox. Not long afterwards, a bibulous woman servant of Northumberland's told some of her friends that the Duke's fourth and only unmarried son, Guilford Dudley, was to marry Margaret Clifford, and added: "Have at the Crown with your leave". The plot was thickening. Northumberland's place as the prospective consort had been taken by his son, and Elizabeth's as the chosen successor to Edward by one of the collateral heirs (although not the one finally chosen), whose gratification at her preferment Northumberland might hope to exploit.

It was Edward's last illness, which began in February 1553, which provided the setting for the final plan. The onset of this illness coincided with the elections for Northumberland's only Parliament. It is generally agreed that Northumberland disputes with Thomas Cromwell the doubtful distinction of having interfered more with Parliamentary elections and proceedings than any other figure of his century. He had begun to do so at the last session, held early in 1552, of the Parliament originally summoned by his predecessor Somerset in 1547. On that occasion vacancies had been filled on the recommendation of the Privy Council, that is to say, under Northumberland's influence, and at least one bye-election, that of one of the Seymours for Reading, had been vetoed by the Government. In 1553 the interference was even more blatant. The Privy Council instructed the sheriffs to return persons recommended by Councillors, and we know that of fourteen individuals so recommended eleven were returned. The House of Commons which met in March 1553 came nearer than any other of its time to being a "packed" assembly.

Why did Northumberland go to such pains to secure a subservient House? Does it mean that he was toying with the idea of forcing through this Parliament some measure designed to promote his succession scheme? It is a possibility. Late in February the Emperor's ambassador reported that the approaching Parliament would give the King his majority. An Act to this effect might well have appealed to Northumberland as a means of strengthening the decision which Edward, at his instigation, would soon be preparing to take, the decision to alter the succession as laid down by his father. If Northumberland did consider this or any other measure, he must have abandoned the idea, probably because of the unwelcome publicity which it would have involved. As things turned out, Parliament met, voted a subsidy, and was dismissed after a session of thirty days only. But with its dispersal Northumberland forwent his one chance of securing Parliamentary sanction or support for his scheme in advance. He could now only hope to have that scheme ratified by Parliament, meeting again perhaps in the autumn, after he had embarked upon it.

With the dissolution of Parliament on 30 Mar. 1553, the scene therefore shifts back to the King and Council, the two instruments of Northumberland's design. Our knowledge of the final phases of that design is largely derived from two documents, both of which have been in print for nearly three centuries.[2] The first and more important of them is the famous "Device" for the succession which Edward wrote out in his own hand, probably about the middle of May 1553. According to this document the crown was to pass, on the King's death and in default of a male heir of his own, to the male heirs of five of the collateral descendants of Henry VIII— Frances Duchess of Suffolk, her three daughters Jane, Catherine, and Mary Grey, and Margaret Clifford—in the order named. Now the most striking feature of this arrangement is that it excludes a woman ruler altogether: both Mary and Elizabeth are left out and the collateral descendants are represented, not in their own persons, but in those of their male heirs. The implication that no woman was fit to occupy the throne was wholly in accordance with the prejudices of the age, and we can

[2] They were first printed by Burnet in his *History of the Reformation in England*, and are most conveniently studied in *The Chronicle of Queen Jane*, ed. J. G. Nichols (Camden Society, 1850), 89 ff.

scarcely doubt that it would have commended itself to the young Edward, conscious as he was of his own, however feeble, masculinity. It was, indeed, precisely this feature which was calculated to give the arrangement a certain specious validity.

But that same feature also meant that the arrangement needed time for its implementation. For at the date when it was drawn up none of the male heirs in question had been born, none of them had, indeed, yet been conceived. Thus, whatever the laws of the realm had to say about the proposed arrangement, the laws of biology were sufficient to gainsay its being carried out in any period short of nine months.

So much for the original "Device". But in the form in which it has come down to us this document bears certain erasures and insertions, in a hand which may be the King's, the purpose of which is clear enough. The crucial alteration occurs in connexion with one of the names enumerated, the name of Lady Jane Grey. Instead of the succession being vested in "the Lady Jane's heirs male", as originally written, it is vested, by means of an erasure and an insertion, in "the Lady Jane and her heirs male". The effect of this simple alteration was to bring into the line of succession, alongside the hypothetical male heirs, one living person, and in so doing to provide against the hiatus which would otherwise occur if Edward were to die before a male heir was born.

Now it is clear that these two arrangements, the first made by the original "Device" and the second by its alteration, correspond to two different estimates of Edward's expectation of life, if not to two different stages

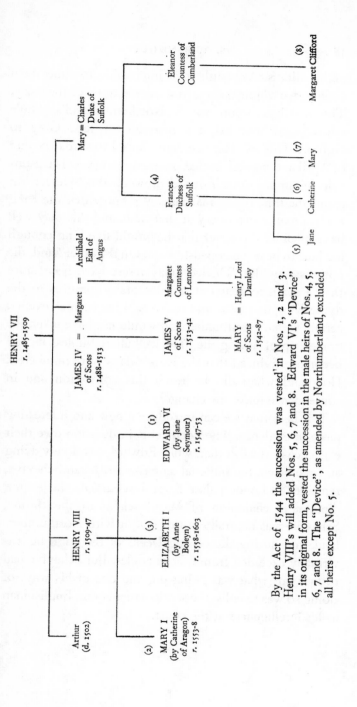

HENRY VII
r. 1485-1509

Arthur
(d. 1502)

HENRY VIII
r. 1509-47

JAMES IV = Margaret = Archibald
of Scots   Earl of
r. 1488-1513   Angus

Mary = Charles
       Duke of
       Suffolk

MARY I
(by Catherine
of Aragon)
r. 1553-8
(2)

ELIZABETH I
(by Anne
Boleyn)
r. 1558-1603
(3)

EDWARD VI
(by Jane
Seymour)
r. 1547-53
(1)

JAMES V
of Scots
r. 1513-42

Margaret
Countess
of Lennox

MARY = Henry Lord
of Scots   Darnley
r. 1542-87

Frances
Duchess of
Suffolk
(4)

Eleanor
Countess of
Cumberland

Jane
(5)

Catherine
(6)

Mary
(7)

Margaret Clifford
(8)

By the Act of 1544 the succession was vested in Nos. 1, 2 and 3. Henry VIII's will added Nos. 5, 6, 7 and 8. Edward VI's "Device", in its original form, vested the succession in the male heirs of Nos. 4, 5, 6, 7 and 8. The "Device", as amended by Northumberland, excluded all heirs except No. 5.

of his illness. Although it is impossible to time them exactly, we can fit them into what we know of the story. The marriage upon which Northumberland's whole scheme was founded, the marriage of Jane Grey to Guilford Dudley, had been announced towards the end of April and was celebrated on 21 May 1553. It is reasonable to suppose that Edward drew up the "Device" at about the time of the marriage. We know that the King made a marked recovery at that time, and this may well have inspired the belief that he would live long enough for Jane to bear the hoped-for son. On the other hand, the optimism of the "Device" may never have been more than a sham to bear out the doctors' assurances to the dying King that he would recover. What is, at all events, certain is that Northumberland would not have taken the grave step of having the "Device" altered unless he had become convinced that the King's days were numbered. How and when did he reach this conviction and in consequence make the change?

It is here that we can introduce a new and interesting piece of evidence. The documents in question owe their existence to the fact that, while Edward was slowly dying at Greenwich, the Imperial ambassador, Jehan Scheyfve, remained in London aloof from the court. As the leading diplomatic champion of Mary's claim to the throne, Scheyfve was naturally out of favour with Northumberland, and during the closing weeks of the reign he was virtually excluded from official circles. But Scheyfve had to find out what was going on, and one of his ways of doing so was to enlist the services of a young Englishman as his intelligencer at the court.

This young Englishman was John Banister. The twenty-year-old son of a minor official in the royal household, Banister was on the threshold of the medical career which was to yield him a modest fame under Elizabeth I and to earn him a place in the Dictionary of National Biography.[3] How he came to purvey news to the ambassador we do not know. But tucked away in a file of Scheyfve's letters, in the *Archives Nationales* at Brussels, there are seven Latin letters which, although unsigned and undated, can with certainty be pronounced to have been written to him by Banister at various dates between 26 May and 21 Jul. 1553. The letters are mostly tantalisingly brief and scrappy, but they do add a little precious information to the meagre record of the last weeks of Edward's life and the brief reign of Queen Jane.

The longest and by far the most interesting of the letters was written on 28 May 1553. After describing the reception of a special French envoy at court on that day— it is this passage which fixes the date of the letter—the writer went on to give the latest news of the King's illness.

> In what concerns our king's health [he wrote] be assured of this, that he is steadily pining away. He does not sleep except he be stuffed with drugs, which doctors call opiates . . . first one thing then another are given him, but the doctors do not exceed 12 grains at a time, for these drugs are never given by doctors (so they say) unless the patient is in great pain, or tormented by constant sleeplessness, or racked by violent coughing. . . . The sputum which he brings up is livid, black, fetid and

[3] Which errs in giving 1540 as the year of his birth. He was born in 1533.

full of carbon; it smells beyond measure; if it is put in a basin full of water it sinks to the bottom. His feet are swollen all over. To the doctors all these things portend death, and that within three months, except God of His great mercy spare him.

Today the Duke called the doctors together and asked them what the king's chances were. With one voice they answered that since this season of the year is kindest to him but yet does nothing to improve him, so likewise when autumn comes it will end his life. The Duke, hearing this, told them not to slacken their efforts nor to cease to pray to God that He should prosper their treatment; meanwhile, he said, you will all be paid your fees every month, at a rate of 100 crowns.

Apart from its first-hand account of the King's symptoms and treatment (given, it should be remembered, by one who was himself a medical student), the value of this letter lies in its revelation of the fact, hitherto unknown, that just one week after his son's marriage to Jane Grey Northumberland sought and received the unanimous verdict of the King's doctors that Edward could not live beyond the autumn. If we assume, as I think we may, that the "Device" for the succession then still stood in the original form in which Edward had copied it, we can surely see in this medical conference of 28 May the ground of Northumberland's drastic decision to have it altered. For if the doctors were right, Edward had no chance of lingering on long enough to give Jane herself, or indeed any of her fellow-claimants, time to produce the indispensable male heir; and the King's death would therefore leave a throne which was not only empty but which, according to the terms of the

"Device", could not be filled. To that problem, once it
arose, there could be, as Northumberland well knew, but
one answer—the accession of the heir named by Henry
VIII, the Princess Mary. His one hope of preventing this,
to him, fatal issue was therefore to "plug the gap"
between the death of Edward and the birth of a male heir
by introducing a living person into the succession: and
this was what he did by his alteration of the "Device" to
include Jane Grey herself.

It was with these few short strokes of the pen that
Northumberland wrote the death-warrants of his son and
daughter-in-law. For it was in this amended form that
the law officers drew up, in the second week of June,
the letters patents declaring the new order of the succession and that on 21 June the document was signed by the
notabilities of the realm. Edward had then only two more
weeks to live, two weeks which Northumberland filled
with the military and naval preparations designed to cow
the country into submission. One thing only he failed
to do, but this one failure was to undo all that he had
done: he failed to capture Mary. When, on 6 July,
Edward breathed his last at Greenwich, Mary, warned
we know not by whom, had already fled from her
Hertfordshire home into Norfolk and was preparing to
stand her ground there.

It was Mary's escape from the trap that had been set
for her which ensured that, after all the care which had
been expended upon it, the succession to the throne of
England in July 1553 should be decided, not by the dead
hand of Henry VIII, nor by the crafty one of Northumberland, but by the English nation. On 10 Jul. 1553,

Jane Grey was proclaimed Queen in London: two days later Mary had herself proclaimed at Framlingham. The country was asked to choose between them. Ten days sufficed the country in making its choice, and in showing that it would take more than the inky blots and rotten parchment bonds of Northumberland's devising to upset the rightful succession to the Tudor throne.

Penry Williams

THE FALL OF ESSEX [1]

During the last decade of the sixteenth century, politics
at the court of Queen Elizabeth were dominated by the
disruptive personality of Robert Devereux, second Earl
of Essex. Brilliant, compelling, thirsty for popularity and
praise, easily unbalanced by slights real or imagined, he
concealed, like Proust's Saint-Loup, an hysterical streak
which drove him on to a seemingly inevitable doom. His
career and his following depended upon the force of his
glittering and unstable personality, for, in spite of the
age and nobility of his family, he was not endowed with
great riches or wide estates. Although some of his
supporters were tenants of the Devereux and some were
his liveried retainers, most were bound to him by the
attraction of his person and the knowledge that he stood
high in Elizabeth's favour. For the Queen was the
dispenser of power, prestige, and riches; and those who
had her ear could retail these things to their followers.

In the close, face-to-face world of the Queen's court,
personal relations were always important, and Elizabeth's

[1] [Copyright © Penry Williams. Originally published in *History
Today*, VII (1957), pp. 721-8.]

affection for her young men was a major part of any
political situation. Politics in this community were partly
—though not of course wholly—the politics of personal
emotions; and the successful politicians were those who
allowed the demands of their careers to guide their
feelings. Essex could never do this: essentially he was a
private person in a public place; his passions were too
violent, too near the surface, to be the servants of his
political conduct.

His rivals, wiser men in this, had formidable qualities
of their own. Sir Walter Raleigh, sailor, poet, and
courtier; Howard of Effingham, later the Earl of Nottingham, a fine sailor and the representative of a great and
ancient family; the Cecils, Lord Burghley and his son
Robert, who in taking from the Queen's shoulders the
heavy task of detailed administration, and in supplying
her with trusted advice, had made themselves as nearly
indispensable to her as any man could be.

Throughout the 1590s Essex competed with these men
for the favour of the Queen and for the rewards that such
favour could bring. Sometimes there was open hostility,
sometimes the appearance of friendship. While Burghley
lived the conflict was kept within reasonable bounds: but
the death of the old Lord Treasurer in 1598 left Cecil and
Essex struggling for his political inheritance. At this
point, before the struggle was resolved, events in Ireland
intervened. The Irish rebels under Hugh, Earl of Tyrone,
had come to control the greater part of the island. The
English Lord Deputy was dead and a successor had to be
found. Essex, although reluctant to leave his enemies a
free hand at court in his absence, was in the end unable

to resist the temptations of military adventure. He left London for Dublin in March 1599.

In the following months Robert Cecil tightened his control upon affairs of state. He himself, already Secretary of State, became Master of the Court of Wards; his brother, the second Lord Burghley, became Lord President of the North; his protégé, John Herbert, became Second Secretary of State. Essex, isolated in Ireland, had not only to hear of his rival's success at court; he had to endure constant criticism from Elizabeth, as his much-vaunted campaign petered out in negotiations with the rebel, Tyrone. Essex's followers, who had entered Ireland in high confidence, began to grumble at the strictures from home, while the Earl himself, ill and desperate, contemplated marching upon London to overthrow his enemies.

When his friends dissuaded him from so extreme a course, he decided instead upon a personal appeal to Elizabeth. At ten a.m. on 28 Sep. 1599, only five days after leaving Dublin, Essex reached the court at Nonsuch, and ran, covered in mud, to the Queen's bedroom, where he found her with her hair, not yet done, hanging about her face. Kneeling, he kissed her hand and her neck, then spoke with her. It seemed that he had succeeded, for he left the presence happily, commenting on the "sweet calm" that he found there after the turmoils of Ireland. Another talk followed at eleven o'clock, and still all was well. At dinner the Earl talked volubly of his Irish campaign to the courtiers and, after his meal, went again to the Queen, to find that her mood had changed. The affectionate welcome had turned to anger.

We shall never know why Elizabeth's mood altered so sharply: but, whatever lay behind the change, it had swift effect. The court hived off into factions, and, on the next day, two separate and hostile groups went in to dinner. Cecil was accompanied by Lord Cobham, his brother-in-law, by the Earl of Nottingham and Sir Walter Raleigh, both of whom had long hated Essex, by the Earl of Shrewsbury, Lord Grey, and Sir George Carew. With Essex walked the young Earl of Rutland, the Catholic Earl of Worcester, Lord Mountjoy, lover of Essex's sister, Lord Rich, that same sister's husband, Lord Lumley, who had been involved in the Ridolfi Plot, Sir William Knollys, Essex's uncle, and Sir Edward Dyer, poet and friend to Philip Sidney. More ominously, his entourage included many knights.

At this critical stage in the struggle for power at court, the final decision lay with none of the rivals, but with the Queen, who, for three days, hesitated before making up her mind. On the day following the Earl's return, a full and secret meeting of the Privy Council was called. Essex heard and answered the Queen's accusation that he had mismanaged the Irish campaign and had returned home without leave; the councillors deliberated for three hours; and Elizabeth, on hearing their conclusions, announced that "she would pause and consider of his answers". She was wise to do so, for Essex was rash, desperate and, above all, popular. London was filled with his followers—disappointed noblemen, adventurous knights, unruly soldiers. Elizabeth could not be certain that she could safely take action against their leader.

But after two days she decided to brave the violence

of his followers. Essex was committed to imprisonment in York House and, gradually, the courtiers began to drift over to the protection of his rival, Robert Cecil. Within ten days, only Lady Scrope, of all the courtiers, dared to speak up for Essex, and the Earl's own servants were afraid even to meet together.

But, if the battle at court was over, the battle outside continued. Returned soldiers, fearing a threat to their livelihood from the Cecilian policy of peace, and Puritan clergy, fighting for their religious beliefs, both attacked the government. Towards the end of November, Elizabeth and her ministers decided to confound their critics. It was usual, at the close of each law-term, for the Lord Keeper to harangue the assembled Justices of the Peace on the need for good government. The occasion provided an assembly of a great part of the political nation, and now the Queen ordered that this gathering should be used for a public defence of her policy. That she should have condescended to explain and justify her actions at all shows how grave the situation was.

Each of the leading ministers tried to prove that Essex had been responsible for the English failure in Ireland during the summer; and the Earl of Nottingham, for so many years his enemy, delivered a personal attack upon the Earl. But the climax of the meeting was, without any doubt, the speech of Robert Cecil. Eloquently and reasonably Cecil justified the peace policy pursued by the Queen, his father, and himself. It was, he argued, quite untrue that this policy ignored the interests of the soldiers: the army would always be protected, for "Her Majesty has a special care of such as be soldiers in deed".

C.T.S.E.——E

It was also quite untrue that Ireland could have been saved, as the war-party suggested, by prompter action; such criticism ignored the efforts of the Queen's government elsewhere, in Scotland, the Netherlands, and France. While carefully avoiding an open attack upon the Earl, Cecil utterly vindicated his own policy.

Yet speeches, however eloquent and convincing, could not resolve the problem. They might quiet public discontent; they could not eliminate Essex's influence. Throughout the ensuing months Essex sought his way back to Elizabeth's favour, encouraged James VI of Scotland to believe that Cecil opposed his succession to the English throne, and urged Mountjoy, the new Lord Deputy in Dublin, to bring over troops from Ireland for the destruction of Cecil, Nottingham, and Raleigh. So long as Essex lived, his fate dominated the court intrigues; and no one could be certain that Elizabeth would keep him from her for ever.

In the face of this threat at least one of his rivals, Sir Walter Raleigh, urged that he be crushed as soon as possible. But the most significant of them, Robert Cecil, behaved very differently. "For my part", he told Francis Bacon, "I am merely passive in this action, and I follow the Queen, and that heavily, and I lead her not". His protestation of neutrality has not always been believed. Some of Essex's followers scribbled slogans against Cecil on the white-washed walls of the court; and some historians, more celebrated, perhaps, for their fantasies than for their accuracy, have chosen to picture Cecil plotting in silence the downfall of his enemies. There is little to support this view. Those closest to the Queen had the best opportunity of seeing what Cecil was doing; Sir Walter Raleigh, impatient to be rid of Essex, thought that Cecil was missing his chance. "If you take it for a good counsel to relent towards this tyrant", wrote Raleigh to Cecil, "you will repent it when it shall be too late".

This is not to say that Cecil held Essex in any affection; in fact, as we shall see, there is good reason to suppose that he detested his rival. But, for the time being, he subordinated his feelings to political necessity. Thirty years before, his father, faced with the conspiracy of the Duke of Norfolk, had shown himself magnanimous when certain of victory. The son no more than the father wished to incur unnecessary hatred; his position was secure and any attempt to depress his enemies further might anger the unpredictable Queen.

Although we can never be certain of Cecil's secret behaviour, it seems probable that his neutrality was genuine and that he used it to conciliate the Earl's followers. When the Queen wished to bring Essex before Star Chamber, Cecil persuaded him to submit to her mercy and thus saved him, for a time, from public trial. When the Earl's wife and sisters were forbidden access to his person, Cecil intervened on their behalf. When Elizabeth threatened to degrade thirty-nine young men who had been knighted by Essex, Cecil won their gratitude by persuading her to rescind the order. Finally, when Essex was brought to a private trial at York House, Cecil treated him courteously and fairly.

This conciliatory policy gradually eased the tension at court during the summer months of 1600. Most of the

Earl's followers cut the ties of loyalty to their leader: Mountjoy, once ready to lead an army to his help, now did nothing; Francis Bacon, once his legal adviser, appeared for the prosecution at his trial. Essex himself, deprived of all his offices, was given liberty to go anywhere except to court, and at first his letters suggested genuine remorse, desire only to see the Queen again: "let my dwelling be with the beasts of the field; let me eat grass as an ox, and be wet with the dew of heaven till it shall please Her Majesty to restore me to my understanding".

Unfortunately Essex was hardly the man to live in retirement; and, in any case, he could not afford to do so. Seriously in debt, he depended for solvency upon his lease of the import duty on sweet wines, which was due to end on Michaelmas Day, 1600. He wrote desperately to the Queen, begging a renewal of the lease, so that he might satisfy the "great number of hungry and annoying creditors, which suffer me in my retired life to have no rest". But Elizabeth granted the lease elsewhere.

Haunted by his debts, angry at his enforced retirement, suspicious of his enemies, Essex lost all political and mental balance. The Queen's refusal to renew his lease not only removed his last hope of dismissing his creditors; it convinced him that he could no longer expect a return to favour and to power. The brilliance and the charm were turned by failure to arrogance, rage, and madness. He "shifteth from sorrow and repentance to rage and rebellion so suddenly", wrote Sir John Harington, "as well proveth him devoid of good reason or like mind".

At Essex House in the Strand, his moderate followers

having deserted him, the Earl was surrounded by about one hundred and twenty "earls, barons, and gentlemen [of] discontented humour". The Earl of Southampton, a court *beau*, had long felt the Queen's displeasure; the Earl of Rutland was young and impulsive, apparently fascinated by Essex; Francis Tresham, a Catholic squire, was excluded from court favour by his religion; Owen and John Salesbury, young swordsmen from the minor Welsh squirearchy, had served with Essex in the wars; Sir Gelly Meyrick, Marshal of the Army in Ulster, was convinced that he could raise a following for the Earl in Wales. Beyond these men in Essex House were the Welsh squires who had long been attached to the Devereux interest; and, in the City of London, there were Puritan divines and their flocks, some of whom regarded Essex as their leader against the established order.

At Essex House, and at Drury House, Southampton's residence, the plans of these heterogeneous rebels were prepared in January 1601. Here the leaders, isolated from the realities of political life, decided to rush upon the court and remove from power Cecil, Nottingham, and Raleigh. Before their schemes were fully concerted, action was forced upon Essex by a summons from the Privy Council. In reply he collected his followers at Essex House on Sunday, 8 February and closed the gates. The Queen seems to have thought no drastic action necessary and sent four Councillors, all of them once friendly to Essex, to warn him to disperse his followers. By now the Earl had gone too far to draw back and his friends were carried away by excitement. The Councillors were kept as hostages while Essex, with two hundred picked men, rode out of the gates and headed eastwards for the City, under the belief that the citizens would rise in his favour.

Essex was mistaken. For Cecil quickly sent into the City his brother, Lord Burghley, with some armed men and a Herald, in order to have the Earl proclaimed a traitor; and the reading of this proclamation was enough to prevent the cautious citizens from rallying to the Earl's cause. Meanwhile Cecil had had time to organise resistance. A barricade of coaches was thrown up in the passage between the court and Charing Cross. Men from the hamlets around Whitehall were quickly assembled and formed into companies.

Now the Earl, having found no support outside his original band, and having heard that troops were marching against him, decided to fall back on Essex House. His way through the streets being barred at Ludgate, he was forced to take to the river with only a few friends. At Essex House he found his last hope gone: the four hostages had been freed. Ineffectual attempts were made to fortify the house before the Queen's troops appeared under Nottingham. For a few hours Essex held out, but at nine o'clock that evening, on the news that ordnance was being brought from the Tower, he yielded.

On the following Friday, the last day of the law-term, the Justices of the Peace were assembled in Star Chamber, according to custom. On this occasion, as in November 1599, the Queen and Cecil used the meeting to justify their treatment of Essex, to provide a curtain-raiser, as it were, to the full-dress trial. Once more it was left to Cecil to undertake the full defence of government. Now that

Essex had condemned himself to certain ruin, Cecil was able to abandon moderation and to allow full liberty to his hatred. In place of the reasoned argument and the calculated fairness of his earlier speech, Cecil delivered a passionate diatribe against his rival. Essex, "more like a monster than a man", had plotted to be King; he had "affected popularity" by attracting the disaffected in religion; he had conspired with Tyrone; and finally he had revealed his intentions of usurping the throne.

There is no scrap of evidence that Essex intended to supplant Elizabeth: but the ministers, convinced that Essex was a menace to stable government, put the safety of the state before the rules of evidence. Cecil, determined that the Earl must die, had written, even before the trial had opened, to Mountjoy in Ireland: "by that time my letters shall come unto you, both he [Essex] and the Earl of Southampton, with some other of the principals, shall have lost their heads". The government's evidence was carefully marshalled and the prosecution was ruthlessly conducted by Sir Edward Coke. The verdict of guilty was a foregone conclusion.

A few days later, on 25 Feb. 1601, between seven a.m. and eight a.m., Essex was brought to the executioner. At his own request his death took place privately; that is to say, it was witnessed by about a hundred noblemen and gentlemen, who were seated on benches near the scaffold. Essex, dressed in a suit of black satin with a black velvet gown, dwelt on the sins of his past life and asked forgiveness for his actions; to the last he denied that he had intended any violence to the Queen. Then he knelt down, prayed to God, and laid his head on the block, his arms stretched out. The axe severed his neck in three blows.

Essex's rebellion has been described both as the last outburst of "the spirit of the ancient feudalism" and as the last revolt of bastard feudalism. It was neither. His fellow-rebels were, in the main, neither tenants nor retainers. They were men barred from court favour, who followed him out of a personal loyalty, founded on the hope that he, the most eminent of excluded courtiers, was the most likely to lead them back to the Queen's good graces. In its prime the Essex faction had by no means consisted only of the excluded and the unfortunate: but those who had kept by him during the eighteen months following Michaelmas Day 1599 were mostly men who had little hope of advancement; either because, like Southampton, they had incurred the anger of the Queen, or because, like the Catholics and the Puritans, their religion opposed them to the establishment. They were, in a sense, rebels without a cause, or, rather, rebels with too many causes. Their discontent could find unity and focus only in Essex. In this the revolt differed both from the Rising of the North in 1569, whose nucleus lay among the Percy and the Neville retainers, and from the Great Rebellion of 1642, when discontent found a solid foundation in Parliament. As a leader of the discontented, Essex was useless, since his own power rested ultimately upon the favour of Elizabeth; in this paradox lay the tragedy of his career, for by rebelling against the Queen's will he was rebelling against the source of his own strength.

D. H. Pennington

A DAY IN THE LIFE OF
THE LONG PARLIAMENT [1]
Tuesday, 16 November 1641:

"November 16, Tuesday, 1641. The Speaker came between nine and ten of the clock."

Sir Simonds D'Ewes, the learned and irrepressible member for Sudbury, sat in his usual place near the Speaker's chair, with his note-book and ink-bottle, and in those words began his record for the day. St Stephen's Chapel was a bare and ill-lit room in the Palace of Westminster, at right-angles to the great thoroughfare of Westminster Hall. Its only movable furniture was the Speaker's chair at the east end, and the table and chairs for the Clerk, Henry Elsing, and his assistant, John Rushworth, who kept the Journals of the House. The four tiers of benches round the walls gave uncomfortable and inadequate seating for members. For spectators there was no provision at all: the little gallery at the west end was used by members, and the only strangers normally admitted were those summoned to the Bar of the House

[1] [Copyright © D. H. Pennington. Originally published in *History Today*, III (1953), pp. 681-8.]

below the gallery. Though many members had adopted regular places for themselves, their position had no connexion with status or allegiance. Pym and Hampden sat near the Bar on the Speaker's left, Hyde and Falkland opposite them, Hesilrige in the gallery.[2] The Privy Councillors, and Court Officials who were members, tended to sit near the Speaker, as their predecessors had done when they were the channel for royal pressure. But in the Long Parliament, especially since the flight of Secretary Windebank, the office-holders were not the representatives, or even necessarily the supporters, of the King.

How many members were present at Prayers on this Tuesday morning we do not know. The House, which in easier times had usually sat from eight a.m. until about noon, was now supposed to meet at nine: but William Lenthall, the Speaker, had several times recently found fewer than the quorum of forty present when he arrived and had taken to being late himself. There were complaints that, in spite of frequent roll-calls and summonses, some two hundred members had not sat since the summer recess. Later in the day, 223 members voted: but to publish a division-list would have been a gross breach of privilege. We can therefore be sure of the presence only of those members named in the Journals, or in private accounts of proceedings. A glance at the connexions and activities of almost any one of them will give a fair idea of the character of the Parliament as a whole.

[2] John Forster in *The Debates on the Grand Remonstrance*, London 1860 (pp. 283-4), works out the places of many other people—including one who was not an M.P. at all.

The first to rise in his place was Sir Walter Erle, one of the four burgesses for Dorset's unique "double borough" of Weymouth and Melcombe Regis. The Erles, like the great majority of the gentlemen chosen for Parliament in October 1640, came from a small and closely-knit landed community of their native county. Though four-fifths of the members sat for boroughs, few lived in them. It was the rise and fall, the rivalries and alliances, of county families that determined who was elected. Sir Walter's principal estate at Charborough was within seven miles of the borough of Wareham, where he held some property, and about as far from Poole. His son, Thomas, was member for Wareham; his brother, Christopher, had formerly sat for Poole and for Lyme Regis. The Erles were related by marriage to the Tren-chards, one of whom, John, was now the other member for Wareham. John's sister was married to Sir John Strangways, member for Weymouth, and father of one of the members for Bridport; his sons-in-law, John Bingham and William Sydenham, were later members of the Long Parliament for Shaftesbury and Weymouth respectively. Almost every county had a similar network of relationships among its members. But of course they did not stop at county boundaries: Walter Erle's sister was married to the brother of William Strode, member for Berealston, two of whose cousins were related by marriage to Pym and through him to at least a score of other south-western members. Thomas Erle's wife was Susanna Fiennes, daughter of Viscount Say and Sele, and through the widespread connexions of the Fiennes family the Erles were related to Hampden, Cromwell, St John,

Holles, and many parliamentary families in the eastern counties. Without going back more than two or three generations, one could link in this way probably half of the members who were in St Stephen's that morning.

Two groups of M.P.s were regarded as being in some respects apart from the rest. One of these consisted of the seventy barristers—"the Lawyers of the House"— among whom was Thomas Erle. The majority were, like him, the sons of landed gentlemen, and all had shared the companionship and teaching of the Inns of Court, where nearly half the landed members had studied for a year or more. But some of the lawyers had risen through their profession from humbler origins, and sat for boroughs of which they were Recorders. A successful legal career was one of the quickest and surest ways to wealth, and several of the richest members enjoyed estates that had been founded by grandfathers or great-grandfathers who were Tudor judges. The other professional group was that of the merchants. The term could be loosely applied to men varying in status from local aldermen like John Baker, the draper, and Simon Norton, the dyer (members for Coventry), to such great national figures as Sir Arthur Ingram and Sir Nicholas Crispe, with a wide range of commercial and financial interests. But "the Merchants of the House", who were collectively added to committees concerned with trade, were primarily the leaders of City companies and the managers and financiers of overseas commerce. One of the members who spoke on 16 November was Samuel Vassall, Alderman of London and M.P. for the City. Like another City member,

John Venn, he was a leading figure in the Massachusetts
Bay Company, one of the Puritan trading and colonising
ventures. This had grown out of the Dorchester Company, and the most prominent of the six Dorset M.P.s
who were among the sponsors of that enterprise was
Sir Walter Erle. Only a minority of the landed members
had so direct a connexion with trade: but very many held
estates that were founded, augmented, or preserved by
merchant wealth.

Sir Walter Erle had risen to move a change in the form
of the daily prayers. The House regularly gave thanks
for its deliverance from the perils of the Spanish Armada
and the Gunpowder Plot. Sir Walter was now proposing
to add the words "and for our deliverances since the
beginning of this Parliament". Henry Marten, the member for Berkshire, whose private life scandalised his
Puritan allies, moved that a Committee be set up to
consider the proposal. But so fascinatingly rare a point
of procedure made it inevitable that the House should
hear from its self-appointed adviser on precedent, Sir
Simonds D'Ewes. A Committee was not necessary "to
draw five or six words which you yourself may draw
(—I spake to the Speaker as is usual—) . . . without
further trouble. And so", he adds with his usual satisfaction, "it was left to the Speaker to do". Sir Walter's
proposal was clearly in tune with the feeling of the
House. It was engaged in detailed examination of the long
catalogue of the misdeeds of Stuart governments that
became the Grand Remonstrance, and the many recent
threats to parliamentary government were clearer than
ever in its memory. But the prayer was not simply about

the political power of Strafford or the religious practices
of Laud. The three deliverances that would now be
brought together were deliverances from the same evil—
the evil to which all others, directly or indirectly, tended.
Sir Walter and his colleagues saw themselves in a world
divided into two. On one side was the community of
prosperous squires, contented tenants, industrious towns-
men—differing sometimes on politics and religion, but
loyal to their King and to the essentials of Protestant
Christianity. On the other side was Popery. Popery was
no mere matter of religious doctrine: it was summed up
perfectly in the memories evoked by the daily prayer: the
invading fleet of the foreigner, and the slinking, under-
ground Englishmen with the gunpowder. It threatened
the whole English way of life. It threatened property
too; for many members knew that their estates, or part
of them, had been monastic land and that its confiscation
under Popery would mean an upheaval in the whole
structure of propertied society.

On all this Parliament was united. But below the
unanimity lay undercurrents of suspicion and resentment.
Thoroughgoing Puritans could not help feeling that
Laud's religion was half way from theirs to Rome, and
that some M.P.s showed too little zeal for the extirpation
of idolatrous ceremonies. The Queen was a Catholic; the
court was a centre of plots and rumours of plots; and the
Protestantism of all connected with it was at least in
danger of contamination. The Long Parliament therefore
had always spent a good deal of its time on the day-to-day
episodes in the campaign against Popery. In the past
fortnight had come news that confirmed its ugliest fears.

A Catholic rebellion had broken out in Ireland; reports of massacres and atrocities were arriving every day; and it was urgently necessary to send an army to restore order. But Pym saw both the dangers and the opportunities of the situation. He would not trust an English or a Scottish army to the command of the "evil counsellors" of Charles. Men and money might be used for encouraging rather than repressing the Irish rebels and the "ill-affected subjects in England". Against strong opposition from an increasingly unified group among his former followers, he had led the House to the revolutionary declaration that, if the King did not employ ministers it approved of, it "would resolve on some such way of defending Ireland from the rebels as may concur to the securing of ourselves. . . . "

Within the last twenty-four hours there had appeared even more immediate cause for alarm. On 15 November Pym had interrupted the debate to report "that there was one attending without who had somewhat to reveal which concerned the safety of divers members of the two Houses". Thomas Beale, a tailor of Whitecross Street, thereupon related, first to a small Committee, then at the Bar of the House, and finally to a Conference of Lords and Commons, a story that rivalled the Gunpowder Plot itself. He had been walking that day in the fields near the Pest House and had overheard a conversation between two unidentified men. As he came within earshot, one of them was regretting that the last plot had failed. But now a hundred and eight people had been appointed, each to kill one Puritan member of the Lords or Commons. Two priests, Father Jones and Father Andrews, were concerned in briefing the assassins. Some of the victims were mentioned by name: Dick Jones was to kill "that rascally Puritan Pym", and four London tradesmen were to deal with the City M.P.s. On the day of the massacre, 18 November, there were to be Catholic risings in various counties; and the confusion would be so great that the expedition to Ireland would have to be called off. If the Catholics prevailed there, "they should not have cause to fear here". Once the conspiracy had been revealed, it was easy to find corroborating evidence. The House heard a story from Portsmouth of new fortifications, directed against attack not from the sea but from the land, of "a Frenchman of the Romish religion" being brought into the garrison as a surgeon, and of regular posts going to the Queen. "The Papists and jovial clergymen thereabouts were merrier than ever." No time could be lost in preparing to frustrate a rebellion that was only three days off. Members handed in to Rushworth the names of prominent Papists in their counties, and a Committee was appointed to arrange for their arrest and to mobilise the Trained Bands. It met forthwith in the Court of Wards and drafted Ordinances, to which the Commons agreed without debate or division, though the Lords had still to consider them.

On this Tuesday morning, therefore, the familiar alarms had acquired unprecedented urgency, and if a night's reflexion had led any members to doubt the plausibility of Beale's story they preferred not to say so. No firm rules of procedure determined what business should come first. Reports on disputed elections often began the day, but though the Committee of Privileges

Miniature of General George Monck by Samuel Cooper,
Windsor Castle.

Reproduced by gracious permission of
Her Majesty The Queen.

DVKE OF YORK

James VII and II, by Sir Peter Lely.

had been meeting in the Star Chamber during the past week to consider the elections at Tewkesbury, it had no report to make. Petitions were also presented early, and in the first months of the Parliament had occupied much of its time. Today, there was only one. Father Browne, a Scottish priest who for months had been a prisoner in the Gatehouse, chose this unpropitious moment to submit a petition. (He had been examined the day before about Jones and Andrews but had denied all knowledge of them.) Sir Henry Mildmay, on behalf of a Committee that was investigating defaults in the payment of poll-money, tried to interest the House in the misdeeds of the under-sheriff of Hampshire who had been summoned to appear at the Bar but had gone out of town. "It came to nothing", says D'Ewes curtly.

The business for which everyone was waiting was opened by Hampden, who had information about the two priests named by Beale. Both were "very dangerous priests": Jones was an agent for the nuns at Douai and was now in the house of the Earl of Worcester, whom members knew as a notorious plotter. Arrangements for searching the houses of the Earl, and of others "justly to be suspected", were left to four members who were Middlesex J.P.s. There was some doubt whether, since a Peer was involved, the Lords ought to be consulted: but it was agreed to act first and settle constitutional proprieties later. Nevertheless, Pym was most anxious at this stage to avoid a quarrel with the Lords. Accordingly a message was sent to the Upper House proposing a "free conference" on the safety of the Kingdom. This procedure had been used regularly in the Long Parliament to enable the two houses to devise legislation and policy in close collaboration. The conferences were usually held in the Painted Chamber, which lay between the two meeting-places, separated from the Commons by the Long Gallery. The house that proposed the conference provided one or two members to act as its "managers" and both appointed "reporters" to bring back an account of the proceedings. On this occasion the Commons chose Pym and Holles for both tasks.

The Lords had spent their morning mainly on hearing a report of the previous day's conference with the Commons, though they had found time also to call for a list of Peers who had not paid their poll-money, and to appoint a Committee to consider the grievances of the Venetian Ambassador, whose mail was being opened. At the conference the Commons outlined their proposals for action, which were duly reported by the Lord Keeper, Littleton. After their midday adjournment the Lords were able to send to the Commons a new contribution to the alarm—a letter from James Stanley, Lord Lieutenant of Lancashire, referring rather vaguely to the great dangers from Ireland and at home. This apparent confirmation of the reality of the plot came at an opportune moment. The Commons, who dispensed with a midday break, had just heard Lawrence Whitaker report on the search of the Earl of Worcester's house: there were no priests or Jesuits there, though someone had told him of a person being conveyed out of a private back door. William Wheeler, another of the J.P.s organising the search, had as little success at Sir Basil Brooke's. Henry Marten came in to admit that he, too, had failed in a similar mission.

But the letter from Lancashire restored confidence. D'Ewes rose to say that though he had formerly doubted Beale's revelations he was now persuaded to believe them.

There was, so far as we can see, not a word of truth in the story of the forthcoming massacre. Its production at this moment met so well the needs of Pym and his associates that they must be suspected at least of careful timing and stage-management. Their principal aim, since Parliament re-assembled in October, had been the passing of the Grand Remonstrance. But there had become evident a growing resistance to three of its most daring features—the attack on the Episcopal Church, the demand for Parliamentary control over the King's ministers, and the appeal to public opinion that was implicit in the proposal to print the document, and indeed in its whole character. The House had now reached the group of clauses on religion, which had been inserted rather awkwardly between the political ones. In a few days it would be ready to vote on the Remonstrance as a whole, and only in an atmosphere of imminent danger was it likely to recover the unity which had been apparent in the attack on Strafford. But as soon as the conference in the Painted Chamber was over, and William Strode, who shared with Pym's son the representation of Berealston, had moved the resumption of the debate on the Remonstrance, it was clear that the opposition had not yet been shocked into silence. "Divers disputes", says D'Ewes, "arose upon that clause which concerned the Common Prayer Book, and many would have had it left out, others would have referred it to the Committee again to review, and so to pass it as it might give satisfaction to all parties". He then adds a note which, because of the offence it might give, he puts into his personal cipher: "We saw that the party for episcopacy was so strong as we were willing to lay the clause aside." Twice during the discussion Pym intervened to bring the conspiracy forward again, moving first that one of the Queen's courtiers, William Crofts, should be brought in custody before the House, and later that Lord Petre's house, "where he was informed there were very dangerous persons", should be searched and guarded. The debate was also interrupted, for quite a different purpose, by Sir Harbottle Grimston, who started an acrimonious argument about the validity of an order made by the Commons for the appointment of "lecturers" in parishes where no sermon was preached. Sir Harbottle had been a close associate of Pym's group, but had developed a grievance against them in one of the earlier Committees and seemed now to be indulging a personal spite by helping the opposition in delaying tactics. He was repeatedly called to order, but the argument went on until it was stopped by the arrival of a message from the Lords agreeing to the proposed searches and appointing the Gentleman Usher of the Black Rod to take part in them. After this the House at last came back to the Remonstrance.

Edward Hyde, now the recognised leader of the defenders of episcopacy, was not satisfied with the deletion of the clause about the Prayer Book: he demanded a new one confirming its existing form. "Many sober men", he argued, were afraid that the Prayer Book would be abolished altogether. (D'Ewes retorted that many of the clergy, who were the real defiers of the Prayer Book, might be sober enough to read it on Sunday but were scarcely so on the other six days.) The episcopal party were now seizing the initiative with good hope of winning a majority that might change the whole tenor of the Remonstrance. Pym tried to revive another alarm about conspiracy by moving that the debate should be suspended for a reading of the depositions taken by the Lords on the "second Army Plot" of June 1641—the scheme to bring troops into London. The proposal was rejected. Rushworth was called on to read out next the most controversial of all the religious clauses—the one which denounced the "Idolatry and Popish ceremonies introduced into the Church by command of the Bishops". Sir Edward Dering, Knight of the Shire of Kent, rose to move its deletion. Dering, a scholarly squire and a frequent and elegant speaker, had been a year earlier among the opponents of both the Court and the Bishops. His conversion to the belief that resistance was now going too far was a startling indication of how much support Pym had lost. In the collection of his speeches which, to the indignation of the other side, he afterwards published, he states his argument against the reference to Idolatry:

What? Plain, flat, formal Idolatry? Name the species of this Idolatry that is introduced by the Bishops . . . and by a *command* of theirs. Who hath read this command? Who hath heard this command? Who hath seen this all-commanded Idolatry and can assign wherein it is? . . . Give me leave to say, no man in the House can charge

and prove all the Bishops, no nor half of them—I dare
say . . . not one among them all, to have issued forth
any one command to Idolatry . . .

Dering's former speeches against episcopacy were
naturally quoted against him by speakers on the other
side. He wanted to reply, but was refused permission to
speak twice on the clause. This time Pym's supporters
would not yield—perhaps because they reckoned themselves to be a majority of the members now present—
and the question was put to the House. The practice was
to take a vote first by voice. The Speaker called in turn
on the Ayes and the Noes, and if he could, gave a
decision. The unsuccessful party might, and on this
occasion did, demand a count. The Speaker had therefore
to nominate two tellers for each side. One party would
then go out of the House and be counted as they returned:
the other would remain in their seats and be counted
there. The Elizabethan custom that the Ayes always went
out had been abandoned, and there were sometimes long
arguments before a division on which side should "go
forth". This time it was the Noes who went. Their tellers
were Dering and Sir Hugh Chomley, member for
Scarborough, who was later to fight first for Parliament
and then for the King. For the Ayes Lenthall chose two
Essex baronets, Sir Thomas Barrington, whose family
had held estates in the county since the thirteenth
century, and Sir Martin Lumley, son of a draper who
became Lord Mayor of London. When the doors were
closed again the Speaker announced the result: the clause
was retained by a majority of 124 : 99. "The episcopal
party", says D'Ewes's cipher note, "failed of their

expectation". They were to fail by a still narrower margin in the celebrated debate on 22 November, when a crowded House carried the Remonstrance as a whole by 159 votes to 148. But for Pym too there was a failure. He had hoped to lead an almost united Parliament in an appeal to the nation against the court. Instead he found himself the leader of one of the two parties that became ever more rigidly distinct until the war began.

He failed also to preserve unity between the two Houses. In the late afternoon Arthur Goodwin, Hampden's colleague as member for Buckinghamshire, was sent to request another conference with the Lords. The proposed agenda included the fortifying of Milford Haven and the Isle of Wight, the removal of a magazine said to be commanded by a Papist, and the arrest of the Recusants already listed. But the most urgent request was that the Lords should join in an Ordinance of Parliament for mobilising the Trained Bands and appointing Essex and Holland as their commanders. This apparently innocent emergency measure would stealthily undermine what the Remonstrance openly attacked; for it threatened two of the King's fundamental powers— his share in Parliamentary legislation and his control of the army. The first proposal for an Ordinance appointing Essex had been made early in November by one of the less prominent supporters of Pym, Oliver Cromwell, member for Cambridge. D'Ewes had supported the notion of legislating by Ordinance in the King's absence with some wholly spurious precedents: but many members recognised that it was a revolutionary step. By making it a regular practice Parliament could—and on

the outbreak of war did—take upon itself all the essential
functions of government. It had already in Pym,
Hampden, Holles, and the other leaders, the embryo of a
Parliamentary ministry usurping the functions of the
King's ministers: and in the work of its numerous
Committees it was performing many of the duties of a
modern Civil Service. At this stage however the Lords
refused to break the unwritten letter of constitutional law.
They had unobtrusively re-worded a proposal brought
to the morning conference for a pardon to Catholics who
betrayed their accomplices, so that it read: "Both Houses
will be humble suitors to the King that they may be
pardoned." Sir John Culpepper and Sir Henry Vane as
managers of the second conference now had to report a
chilly reception of the new proposals. When the Lords
had heard these they withdrew to their own chamber for
discussion, and returned to the conference with answers
that accepted outright only one of the Commons' sugges-
tions. The all-important Ordinance was not to be considered until the next day. Eventually the Lords contrived
to make the power of the two commanders depend on
commissions they already held from the King, and to
incorporate some of the other suggested measures in a
normal Bill.

It was nearly five o'clock when the conference ended,
and the Commons agreed to postpone discussion of the
Lords' reply until next morning. So ended an important,
but not an outstanding, day in this most eventful of all
Parliaments. For the rest of the year sittings were often
even longer. Lenthall, despite occasional respites when
the House resolved itself into a Grand Committee, pro-

tested that seven or eight hours every day was too much for him. Other members were free to come and go at will though before the great debate of 22 November the Sergeant was sent out with the mace to round up those who were strolling in Westminster Hall. Some tried occasionally to insist on the House rising when it was dark, and once pressed to a division their objection to candlelight. But in general the House accepted readily enough the magnitude of its work and the prolongation of its hours. It was still possible in November 1641 to hope that the crisis would pass and members return in peace to their homes and estates. They could hardly foresee that in April 1653, the survivors of the turmoils would still be in St Stephen's when the member for Cambridge arrived with his musketeers to "put an end to their prating".

A. H. Woolrych

THE COLLAPSE OF THE
GREAT REBELLION [1]

How long before the Restoration began the great surge of enthusiasm which welcomed Charles II home to England? From the pages of Pepys and Clarendon and many a lesser witness, its warmth still glows across three hundred years. Was it the release of a national devotion to monarchy and the Stuarts which only force had repressed during the long years of Puritan rule? So all Royalists assumed, and up to a point rightly; a plebiscite would probably have declared for the King at any time after the Civil War. But sentiment is one thing; a passion strong enough to unite men in effective action is rarer, and in this case only arose during that final autumn and winter when the quarrelling heirs of the Long Parliament forfeited the very capacity to govern. It was a response to anarchy; the King returned only when the revolution had collapsed from within.

To this process the professed Royalists contributed very little. The strength of the King's cause was not to

[1] [Copyright © A. H. Woolrych. Originally published in *History Today*, VIII (1958), pp. 606-15.]

be measured in loyal toasts drunk in private or vague offers of future service, and Royalist enterprises against Commonwealth and Protectorate tell a sad story of divisions, jealousies, broken promises, baseless expectations of popular support, and a steadily growing wariness among the old Cavaliers. As for the many others who washed their hands of regicide or grumbled at taxes and redcoats, few were ready to face the cost, in violence and disorder, of exchanging Cromwell's rule for the King's. So long as government kept the peace and protected property, nothing could be so bad as a renewal of civil war.

Cromwell's death gave only short-lived encouragement to the King's friends; Richard's quiet accession was nowhere questioned and widely welcomed. Richard Baxter tells how he and his fellow-Presbyterians, "that had called his father no better than a traitorous hypocrite, did begin to think that they owed him subjection". Since providence for so many years had blighted every enterprise of the house of Stuart (he reasoned), it was surely time to remember that God was more concerned that government itself should subsist than with the particular persons or forms through which it was exercised. Even the Royalists, the French ambassador reported, were glad to persuade themselves that honour no longer demanded their resistance.

Richard's rule appealed to men of substance because it eschewed fanatical extremes in church and state, and emphasised the conservative trends of his father's later years. Moderation, however, was not enough. He brought to his task sincerity, a good presence, blameless morals, and the qualities of an easy-going, likeable country squire. But the precarious balance of interests left at Oliver's death called for constant, positive direction at the centre, and neither Richard nor the second-rate men of his Privy Council could provide it. In the Parliament which met in January 1659 he could have commanded the support of a considerable majority, yet for lack of governmental leadership and management in the House the republican politicians who had disrupted Oliver's two Parliaments were allowed to "addle" this one too.

Richard's gravest weakness was his lack of standing in the army. The officers scarcely knew him, but they felt they had a much stronger claim to guide Oliver's successor than the conservative civilians whom he obviously preferred—Secretary Thurloe in particular, and men with Royalist backgrounds like Lord Broghil, Viscount Fauconberg, Sir Charles Wolseley, and William Pierrepont. Chief among the officers were Richard's brother-in-law Lieutenant-General Charles Fleetwood, a pious, suggestible enthusiast whose political concepts hardly went beyond the catch-phrases of the Saints, and his uncle by marriage Major-General John Desborough, a coarser-grained, more resolute military careerist. With these and the other "grandees" (such as Berry, Sydenham, and Kelsey) who forgathered at Wallingford House, Fleetwood's London residence, thwarted ambition mingled with genuine disapproval of the reactionary tendencies in Richard's government and Parliament. But the commonwealthmen of the army, who by this time included most of the junior officers, had come to view the whole Protectorate as an apostasy, a backsliding from "those virgin days" when they had been the instruments of God's victories, not of worldly pomp and ambition. Scores of sermons and pamphlets reiterated the cry that "the Good Old Cause" was being betrayed by crypto-Royalists and other self-seekers, and they rose to it fanatically. Soon they dominated the whole army. The commanders at Wallingford House, feeling their authority slipping from them, weakly sought a reconciliation with the republican Parliament-men; the Protectorate was falling before a "confederated Triumvirate of republicans, sectaries and soldiers".[2] The end came on 21 April, when Fleetwood summoned the regiments about London to St James's and Richard ordered a counter-rendezvous at Whitehall. Richard, deserted by all but a handful of troops, was forced to dissolve the Parliament.

The generals had hoped to maintain a puppet Protectorate, but republican propaganda had convinced most of their subordinates that they could only recover God's favour for their cause by putting the clock back to a time before their fall from grace; they must restore the Commonwealth as it had been before Cromwell violated it. They had their way. On 7 May the little remnant of the Long Parliament, soon known everywhere as the Rump, took up the reins of government as though six years' eclipse had been a month's adjournment.

Somewhat uncomfortably, the grandees acquiesced. With them now was John Lambert, whom the Council of Officers had reinstated by acclamation. Most brilliant of Cromwell's generals, and still just under forty, his

[2] William Prynne, *The Republicans and others spurious Good Old Cause . . . anatomized* (1659).

dash and skill in battle were keenly remembered, while all he had lost, by challenging Cromwell over the offer of the crown, redeemed—for the commonwealthmen— the major part he had played in removing Barebone's Parliament and erecting the Protectorate. The year 1659 sharpened his flair for political manœuvre and deepened his reputation for intrigue; the scope of his ambition, like his religion, can still only be guessed. While Fleet-wood and Desborough vacillated, he had worked for the overthrow of the Protectorate single-mindedly, allying closely with the republicans in Richard's Parliament and probably helping behind the scenes to inflame the army. Though the officers acclaimed Fleetwood as Commander-in-Chief, Lambert was henceforth the dominant personality among them.

The restored Parliament, however, saw no need to make concessions to any of them. The generals had failed to impose terms on it before it reassembled, and when Lambert presented their requests a week or so later, it simply shelved those articles which were intended to maintain the army's political initiative and independence. It went further, and gratuitously offended them. Slighting the Commander-in-Chief, it retained direct authority over the appointment and promotion of officers, and required every one of them within reach of London to receive a new commission at the hands of the Speaker. It established a powerful militia as a counterpoise to the army. Soon only two considerations kept the grandees' resentment in check: the junior officers' continued devotion to the Rump, and the common knowledge that a Royalist rising was imminent.

The Royalists' prospects were brighter now, in so far as the Rump was much more widely disliked than Richard's Protectorate had been. The country had had enough six years ago of these oligarchs who masqueraded as the sovereign people's representatives, and had now recovered power by exploiting the radical enthusiasms of soldiers and sectaries. This made them doubly obnoxious to the moderate Parliamentarian gentry, the Presbyterians—in the current political sense—who had never aimed further than a limited or "mixed" monarchy, and hated swordsmen, regicides, fanatics, and all other disrupters of social and political order. Such men the Cavaliers counted on enlisting, and perhaps some powerful ex-Cromwellians too: General Monck and Admiral Montagu, for example. They would declare at first only for a free Parliament.

In August all these hopes were dashed. Instead of simultaneous risings in a score of counties, only one party, drawn from Cheshire and Lancashire, remained in arms after the first night, and these four thousand men broke and fled as soon as Lambert brought an adequate force against them. That took nearly three weeks, for the Commonwealth's forces, committed as they were in Scotland, Ireland, and Flanders, were thin and scattered outside London. Good intelligence and prompt countermeasures probably doomed the rising before it started, but equally fatal to it was the spirit of jealousy, faction, and cautious self-interest which it exposed among the Royalists themselves. In Cheshire, the Presbyterian gentry and clergy gave it both leadership and numbers, but elsewhere the old mistrust between Presbyterian and

Cavalier remained too strong. Elsewhere, too, the militia proved as loyal to the Commonwealth as the regular forces. Volunteers came forward readily for the defence of London, Gloucester, and other towns, and after Lambert's easy victory the Cheshire countryfolk helped to round up the fugitives. These were not the symptoms of an overwhelming national desire for the King's return.

In the long run, however, the Royalist defeat actually hastened the Restoration, for it unleashed dissensions between army and Parliament which ruined both. The Rump, while scorning to conciliate the Presbyterians, had failed to pay the soldiers their arrears, and alienated the sectaries by voting to continue tithes. In the army, the taste of action had revived something of the old solidarity; all ranks saw themselves as the saviours of the good old cause, and reacted aggressively to any hint of a slight. They advanced provocative claims which were answered with a fatal blend of arrogance, suspicion, and panic.

For this suicidal quarrel Sir Arthur Hesilrige must share the responsibility with the army leaders. He had always been a promoter of extreme measures, ever since the attainder of Strafford, the Root-and-Branch Bill and the Militia Ordinance. Though not a regicide, he had been one of the two or three dominant politicians of the Commonwealth, and had carved a great estate for himself out of the Bishopric of Durham. His *idée fixe* was that nothing—King, Protector, House of Lords, Cromwellian Upper House or the "select senate" which the officers were currently demanding—must set bounds to the supreme authority of the people's representatives, even

Anthony Cooper, first Earl of Shaftsbury.
Portrait after Greenhill.

William III, by Gottfried Schalcken.
Walker Art Gallery, Liverpool.

when those representatives were a small fraction of a Parliament elected nineteen years ago. He is the classic example of the politician who will see no difference between the professions of his party and its practices. His intransigent nature, his sour, irascible temper, his dangerous elations in moments of success and his vindictiveness towards opponents were liabilities to his cause. To him, Ludlow wrote, "liberality seemed to be a vice".

The only serious challenger to Hesilrige's leadership of the Rump was Sir Henry Vane. Both men were skilled Parliamentary tacticians, pillars of the Commonwealth and persistent anti-Cromwellians. But whereas Hesilrige's Puritanism was of a lowish temperature—he now favoured a broad Presbyterian establishment—Vane was a hero of the sects (though he belonged to none of them), and was deeply influenced by the mystical and millenarian strains in contemporary religious experience. Hesilrige was essentially a Whig,[3] and all his rhetoric about the sovereignty of the people served merely to counter any claim to authority but that of the assembly which he had learned to dominate. Vane by contrast told the Rump that the people were mad, and not to be trusted with supreme authority; he would have restricted full citizenship to the Saints and the army, and balanced the people's representatives with a senate or "Council of Elders", appointed for life as guardians of the good old cause. Vane strove constantly to mitigate the Rump's

---

[3] For Professor Trevor-Roper's stimulating justification of this anachronism, see *Essays Presented to Sir Lewis Namier* (1956), pp. 15-18.

provocations to the army, but his following in the House was much smaller than Hesilrige's.

The news of the victory in Cheshire inspired a motion to promote Lambert to Major-General. Hesilrige crushed it. A month later Lambert's officers, now at Derby, sent up a petition reviving the demands he had presented last May, and further asking that Fleetwood should be permanently appointed Commander-in-Chief, Lambert General and second-in-command, and Desborough and Monck chief commanders of the horse and foot respectively. Fleetwood showed this to Hesilrige, who divulged it to the House in a manner calculated to raise the utmost antagonism to the army. Lambert's guilt was assumed, and it was even moved to send him to the Tower, though there was and is no real evidence to connect him with the petition. But the Rump would have no more generals, and ordered Fleetwood to admonish his officers.

It was now hoped that the Council of Officers would mend matters with an address of loyalty to the Parliament. Unfortunately, most of the junior officers who had hitherto been its champions now shared Lambert's resentment. The "Humble Representation" which Desborough presented on 5 October not only vindicated the Derby petitioners, but added fresh demands to those of last May, aiming like those at increasing the army's political independence. A week later the Rump learned that Lambert and his colleagues had been writing to the regiments (including Monck's in Scotland) for signatures to this inflammatory document, even after its presentation to Parliament. As if daring the army to violence, it immediately cashiered Lambert, Desborough, and seven others who had signed the offending letters, and revoked Fleetwood's commission as Commander-in-Chief.

The result was another reckless trial of strength, this time to see whether the troops would obey Lambert or the Parliament. They came near to fighting in the streets —much nearer than in April—but the day ended with Lambert in command and the doors of the Parliament-house once more closed by the soldiery. "In all the hurly burly the streets were full, everyone going about their business as if not at all concerned", wrote an eye-witness, and the City, when the Rump called upon its militia for help, refused to meddle. The Venetian resident marvelled at the phlegm of the English people, who could come through such frequent changes and commotions without bloodshed,[4] and it is true that for some weeks city and nation remained remarkably unmoved.

But this apathy merely registered the unpopularity of Rumpers and soldiers alike, and it was not to last much longer. For the moment, it might be well to see what Monck would do, for he had declared promptly and strongly for the Rump, and his threatened intervention brought Lambert hurrying north with much of the English army.

Meanwhile, after ten days' groping which showed at least how unpremeditated their *coup* had been, the Council of Officers had vested political authority in a Committee of Safety, which joined Vane, Ludlow, Whitelock, and a few lesser politicians with the army leaders. They

[4] He attributed their political inconstancy to their deplorable weather.

negotiated anxiously with Monck, and their hopes rose when his commissioners signed a treaty on 15 November whereby a new Parliament was to be summoned, its form to be determined by a General Council representing all the regiments in England, Scotland, and Ireland, and the fleet. But Monck also wrote to the City authorities inciting them to resist the violators of Parliament while he held down their forces in the north, and he refused to ratify the treaty without further negotiation. He was indeed using cold war tactics to gain the time he needed for purging and consolidating his forces.

And now came the first taste of sheer anarchy. Behind it lay many months of high prices and bad trade, now worsened by chronic political instability. For fear of the soldiery, goldsmiths moved their valuables out of town; lack of livelihood made the lesser citizens rebellious; riots sent the shutters up on thousands of shops. London, "the master wheel by whose motions the successive rotations of all the lesser must follow", was naturally most affected, but did not suffer alone.

Associations sprang up around mid-November, in London and half-a-dozen counties, to refuse payment of taxes, so that troops had to help in their collection. With the soldiers already forced, in some parts, to live at free quarter for lack of pay, incidents were inevitable, and soon they multiplied. At the same time the great courts of Common Law at Westminster closed in mid-term because the judges' commissions from Parliament had expired; the rule of law was visibly in abeyance. The apprentices, watermen, and other elements of the London mob were getting out of control. Petitions for "a full and

free parliament" circulated freely, and all and sundry
were pressed to sign them.

Against such petitioning the Committee of Safety
soon issued a proclamation, and required the Lord Mayor
to publish it. He insisted on first consulting the City's
Common Council, but while it was sitting, early on the
morning of 5 December, the Parliament's serjeant-at-
arms arrived with a troop of horse and proceeded to read
the proclamation before the Old Exchange. He did not
get far. Apprentices pelted the party with tiles from the
roofs and lumps of ice from the gutters, and drove it
back in disorder to St Paul's. Soon the streets filled, the
shops closed, and a great popular demonstration against
the army was only checked when two regiments marched
in under Desborough and Hewson. They broke down
one of the gates which the rioters had closed, but the
mob reviled and stoned them until they finally opened
fire, killing at least two citizens and wounding more.
Popular indignation and propaganda soon inflated this
"massacre" into a minor Peterloo.

The same day, the apprentices presented to the
Common Council their petition for a free Parliament, to
be attained either by electing a new one or restoring the
"secluded members", the moderate, monarchist Presbyterians whom the army had turned out eleven years ago.
Either course would have brought back the King, as all
knew. The City fathers thanked them, and appointed a
strong committee to secure the capital's peace and safety
and confer when necessary with Fleetwood "for preventing misunderstandings between the City and army".
There was no recognition here of the Committee of

Safety; the City's own "committee of safety" treated with Wallingford House on equal terms. During an interregnum like the present, they said, their Lord Mayor ought rather to give law than receive it from others. He and the Court of Aldermen declined a summons to Whitehall on the 6th, and merely sent seven of their number to announce the measures the City was taking. The coroner's court which sat on the victims of the riot brought in a verdict of wilful murder against Hewson. The Common Council prepared to assert its own control over London's trained-bands, despite the Committee of Safety's recent appointment of militia commissioners for the city.

Meanwhile, Hesilrige and two Rumper colonels had secured Portsmouth, and their success stimulated further defections from the Committee of Safety among the forces in Wiltshire, Sussex, Leicester, and Yorkshire. London was seething. On 11 December, a Republican plot to seize the Tower was discovered, and the Lord Mayor called out several thousand householders in arms against a rumoured rising by the sectaries. Two days later came warning of another insurrection. Calamy and other Presbyterian ministers prayed and preached openly for the King. "The army men are almost watched off their legs", it was reported; officers dare not wear their swords in the City for fear of affronts, and soldiers who ventured alone into side-streets were beaten up. Hundreds of shops now stayed shut.

The army leaders' only hope now was that the representative General Council of the Army, which had assembled—very incomplete—on the 6th, would produce some blueprint of a Commonwealth which would restore unity to all who still opposed the rising tide of monarchy. After a week it voted that a new Parliament, consisting of two elected assemblies—Senate and Commons—should meet in January, and that twenty-one Conservators of Liberty should watch over the "Fundamentals" of the constitution. This scheme evidently gave pause to the City authorities, for they turned cool towards the latest petition for a free Parliament and shelved the project of raising their own militia. They acquiesced in the posting of large military guards at the gates and other key points, and ordered all householders to keep their sons and apprentices indoors.

This raised an outcry that the City was being betrayed by its masters, and that evening the Lord Mayor's coach was stoned. The eager young railed against their cautious seniors; apprentices, journeymen, watermen, and all who had little to lose cried shame upon the wealthy patriciate whose property—some said their large purchases of confiscated lands—made them anxious to avert disorder at any price.

But another week of reverses for the Committee of Safety emboldened the City authorities once more. Monck, they heard, had advanced his quarters on 8 December to Coldstream on the Tweed. On the 13th, Vice-Admiral Lawson wrote to them inviting their co-operation in restoring the Rump, and sailed with his fleet from the Downs up to Gravesend. A *coup* in Dublin aligned the army in Ireland on the same side. There were abortive insurrections for a free Parliament in Bristol,

Taunton, and Colchester. In London a Royalist rising was nipped in the bud on the 18th, thanks to a warning from the Lord Mayor, but that was his last gesture of collaboration. Two days later, stung by many angry taunts, the Common Council issued a declaration that they had never accepted the limitations under which the army proposed to call a Parliament, and that they would "endeavour, all they lawfully may, the speedy convening of a free Parliament to sit and act without interruption or molestation by any persons whatsoever".

Next day the annual election of a new Common Council took place, and the City's choice heartened the King's friends. News also came that the forces which Fleetwood had sent to recapture Portsmouth had gone over to the defenders. The 2,500 troops still in London were by now so demoralised by the citizens' execrations, so exasperated by lack of pay, and so worked upon by republican colonels who had been cashiered but not silenced, that their obedience was increasingly doubtful. Despair reigned in the Committee of Safety. Vane had now parted company with the officers, Fleetwood could do little but pray and weep, while Desborough and others contemplated shutting themselves in the Tower for a last stand. The Common Council voted on the 23rd to organise six militia regiments immediately, with officers commissioned under the City's common seal, and sent commissioners to treat with Lawson, with Hesilrige, and with Fleetwood and the Speaker for the calling of a free Parliament. On Christmas Eve, with Hesilrige on the march from Portsmouth at the head of considerable forces, the regiments in London paraded before the Speaker's house and acclaimed him as their general. Fleetwood threw in his hand, remarking "that the Lord had blasted them and spit in their faces, and witnessed against their perfidiousness". The Rump returned in triumph two days later.

But how many would rest content with this outcome? Not the City, which ordered posts and chains to be set up for the defence of its streets and reasserted its right to dispose of its own militia. A formal petition to the Rump for the readmission of the secluded members was drafted and approved, and though the Common Council suspended it at the last moment (on the 29th), it sent a copy by its sword-bearer to Monck, and went ahead with settling the six regiments.

Then on the 30th Lord Fairfax, emerging from ten years' retirement to give Monck vital support, headed a formidable rising in Yorkshire. Many regular troops came in to him who revolted from Lambert out of loyalty to the Rump; so did the Presbyterian gentry, whose declared faith in parliamentary rule privately posited a restoration of monarchy. Similarly ambiguous movements were afoot in the midlands, and in all the multiform protest against the army's usurpation it was far from clear which strain—Republican, Presbyterian or Cavalier—would emerge uppermost.

The issue really hinged on George Monck. His vanguard crossed the Tweed on New Year's Day unopposed—Fairfax's capture of York and the news of the Rump's return had broken Lambert's army—and his march soon became a triumphal progress. He knew before he started that Lambert was cracking and the

Rump already restored, and he had no orders to bring his army south; the Speaker only sent them later, to put a good face on a *fait accompli*. Had Monck already embraced the King's cause, as his apologists afterwards claimed? It is more than doubtful, and certainly more than the King knew. He had first intervened to dissociate himself from the blunderings of the Wallingford House crew, and perhaps to counter a possible bid for dictatorship by Lambert; his march to London surely conveyed that he did not trust Hesilrige and the Rumpers very much further.

But he professed the most scrupulous obedience to them. The gentry of several counties presented him with their declarations for a free Parliament, declarations which multiplied during January and amounted to a concerted repudiation of the Rump's authority by much of England. They were variously addressed to Parliament to Monck, and to the Lord Mayor and City of London, and many added a refusal to pay any taxes until their counties were fully represented at Westminster. Monck always replied by urging acceptance of whatever Parliament should settle, and published an elaborate reply to his countrymen of Devon, arguing that the growth of religious variety and the traffic in confiscated lands since the Civil War had made monarchy—which the secluded members aimed at—insupportable to the nation. It was paradoxical that the Committee of Safety, which had promised a new Parliament of a kind, had been hissed off the stage, while Monck, who professed an obstinate adherence to the Rump, was cheered as a potential liberator.

But surely he meant more than he declared? So everyone guessed, not least at Westminster. The Rump, shrunk
still further by the exclusion of Vane and others who had
acted with the Committee of Safety, now split between
diehard republicans like Hesilrige, who thoroughly dis-
trusted Monck, and opportunists like Speaker Lenthall
and Sir Anthony Ashley Cooper who shared his intention
of riding out whatever storm might be coming. These
men persuaded the House to comply with his request
that the regiments about London—now mostly under
strongly republican colonels—should be removed[5] and
widely dispersed, to make room for his own. This crucial
decision cost four hours' debate, but it meant that when
Monck entered London on 3 February, the Rump was
at his mercy.

Was it to test him that five days later it ordered him
to punish the City—to uproot its posts and chains, take
down its gates and arrest its leading citizens? The
Common Council, discouraged by Monck's reply to its
addresses, had held its hand during January, but when
on arrival he still appeared to support the Rump's
pretensions, it decided to act without him. On 8 February
a clear majority pressed to forbid the collection in
London of the new taxes voted by the Rump, which took
next day the drastic decision to dissolve the Common
Council and subdue the City by military force.

Monck's troops set about their odious task before a
shocked and sullen populace. After a day of it he asked

[5] Two of them mutinied, refusing to leave London without their
pay. Another regiment mutinied at Gravesend. The promise of
discipline was almost enough in itself to make Monck welcome.

for a respite, both for the City and for his protesting officers and men, but the Rumpers brusquely ordered him to continue until gates and portcullises were totally destroyed. Then on the 11th he turned on them. In a famous letter he reproached them for encouraging the contentious demands of the sectaries, failing to banish Lambert and Vane from London, and allowing abettors of the Committee of Safety to remain in Parliament and army. He gave them till Friday to issue writs for elections to all vacant seats in the House. Then he summoned a meeting of the proscribed Common Council. The City went mad with joy; bells rang from every steeple, bonfires sprang up that night in every street, and before them the citizens spitted every steak they could lay hands on, to signify "the roasting of the Rump".

That body retaliated by terminating Monck's appointment as Commander-in-Chief and putting the army under five commissioners, including Hesilrige and other "diehards". But even without this provocation, his next step must have been clear. From Cornwall, Exeter, and Abingdon reports had come during January of riotous demonstrations for a free Parliament, and Bristol had risen early in February. On the 12th, Fairfax and the Yorkshire gentry sent up a threatening declaration, and elsewhere too the leading landowners prepared to back their demands with action. Peace could hardly have been preserved had they been thwarted much longer.

Monck stayed ten more days in the City, conferring with the secluded members and trying to bring the leading Rumpers to accept their readmission. Then on the 21st, when negotiation had failed, his guards quietly let eighty of them into the House—enough easily to outvote the Rumpers—and the long weeks of uncertainty were over. For the second time in eleven days London celebrated with bonfires and bells, and toasts to Charles II were drunk in the streets.

For the Restoration was indeed a certainty. The transformed Parliament set up a thoroughly monarchist Council of State and enacted its own dissolution. There could only be one outcome to the general election which followed. Monck's neat surgery had probably saved a more dangerous blood-letting; he had opened a way through the dismal political *impasse* for the surge of Royalist feeling to flow safely to its fulfilment. He would never have betrayed the Protectorate, but when its destroyers divided their own supporters—officers, radical Independents, sectaries, commonwealthmen—with such meaningless quarrels that the soldiers threatened to make a ring for their officers to fight in, he decided he must act. Once committed, he gradually found his course determined by the sheer force of public opinion—a public opinion converted to ardent Royalism when ordered government deteriorated to the point where resistance became less ruinous than the continuance of misrule. All could unite in turning back to the old foundations, since upon them alone now the rule of law could be re-established.

J. P. Kenyon

THE EXCLUSION CRISIS [1]

On 13 Aug. 1678, King Charles II was strolling in
St James's Park when he was accosted by Christopher
Kirkby, an amateur chemist whom he knew slightly.
Kirkby warned him that the Catholics had hired two
assassins to shoot him, and that, failing this, the Queen's
physician, Sir George Wakeman, would poison him.
Charles was blankly incredulous, but he agreed to meet
Kirkby's informant, Dr Israel Tonge, that evening at
Whitehall. Tonge, the Rector of St Michael's, Wood
Street, was a clergyman of some distinction, but his
personal eccentricities and his rather queer reputation
did not inspire confidence. He produced a paper in
forty-three sections, outlining a conspiracy by the
Society of Jesus, encouraged and financed by the Pope
and the King of France, to assassinate Charles and put
his Catholic brother, James, Duke of York, on the
throne. Ireland was to be appropriated by France, a large
army was to be raised by the Catholic nobility in
England, and the Protestant Church was to be suppressed.

[1] [Copyright © J. P. Kenyon. Originally published in two parts in
History Today, XIV (1964), pp. 252-59 and pp. 344-9.]

The King regarded the whole document as an impudent fabrication; and he was confirmed in this opinion when Tonge declined to reveal who had drawn it up. The Lord Treasurer, the Earl of Danby, was much more wary: he dare not risk the story's being true. But after more than two weeks' investigation he had uncovered nothing more, and he was losing patience when Tonge hastily produced further "evidence" in the form of a packet of incriminating letters sent to Father Bedingfield, the Duke of York's confessor, purporting to come from other English Jesuits. These letters were such blatant forgeries—they could never be produced in the treason trials that followed—that James at once insisted that they be submitted to the Privy Council on 28 September. But this attempt to expose the "Plot" backfired. For Tonge at last brought forward his informant, Titus Oates, a renegade Catholic of homosexual tendencies, whose glib effrontery, backed by the undisputable fact that he had spent some time in Catholic Spain and at the Jesuit seminary at St Omer, stampeded most of the Council. A wave of arrests followed, among them that of Edward Coleman, the Duchess of York's secretary.

How much longer this farce would have proceeded on Oates's unsupported word, plus a few incompetent and impertinent forgeries, is a matter for speculation. Probably not for long. He was not the first man in Charles II's reign to raise the cry of a Popish Plot, and the others are long forgotten. But there now came two events that handsomely confirmed his testimony. When Edward Coleman was arrested on 29 September, his papers were searched, and among them was some correspondence, mostly from the year 1674, between him and various European Catholics, including Fr La Chaise, Louis XIV's famous Jesuit confessor. The correspondence was mainly concerned with a vague project to re-establish Catholicism in England.

The Clerks of the Council were still transcribing and translating Coleman's letters when the Government was informed of the disappearance of Sir Edmund Godfrey, a London magistrate of considerable distinction, widely respected and well known both in Court and City. Outside the Court he was one of the very few people to whom Oates and Tonge had communicated their story. He disappeared on 12 October, and he was found five days later on Primrose Hill, near Hampstead; he had been strangled, then transfixed by his own sword. Many ingenious theories have been put forward to account for these facts, but none of them is entirely satisfactory. In October 1678 not one man in a thousand even entertained the idea that he had not been murdered by the Catholics.

Parliament reassembled on 21 October after the summer recess, and was presented with the "evidence" as it then stood. An examination of Coleman's letters and the interrogation of Oates—now the hero of the hour—were enough to convince the House of Commons "that there had been and still is a damnable and hellish Plot, contrived and carried on by popish recusants for the assassinating and murdering the King, and for subverting the government and rooting out and destroying the Protestant religion". The atmosphere at Westminster was hysterical: the cellars were searched for gunpowder, and a committee was hastily appointed to examine the royal firework-maker, whose foreign name (Choqueux) and residence in the Savoy were enough to put him under grave suspicion. The Upper House was not immune, and it was before a Lords' Committee appointed to investigate Godfrey's murder that the next arch-perjurer, William Bedloe, first appeared. Those he first accused had unshakeable alibis, but he was luckier at the second attempt, when he named Miles Prance, a Catholic silver-smith already arrested on suspicion. With the ready assistance of his inquisitors Prance made up a circum-stantial tale of how he, with a certain Green, Berry, and Hill, two of them servants at Somerset House, the Queen's residence, had murdered Godfrey and, after many adventures, found a suitable resting place for him on Primrose Hill. This was enough to hang Green, Berry, and Hill the following February, and so turn Prance into a committed liar, anxious at all costs to support Oates and Bedloe. "Innumerable small fry of informers", to quote David Ogg, "filled in the few gaps left in the gigantic edifice".

The general acceptance of the Plot is difficult to explain to twentieth-century readers: but in the condi-tions of the seventeenth century there was nothing astonishing about it. Several important men helped it on its way: Danby hoped to demonstrate that he was hard on the Catholics; the Parliamentary Opposition that he was soft, while James, with his usual naïvety, expected that the more publicity the Plot received the more ludicrous it would appear. He did not reckon with the fierce hatred of Popery engendered in the people by

C.T.S.E.——H

Elizabethan propaganda, a hatred so fierce that a clergy-man could be impeached in 1628 for arguing that the Bishop of Rome did not always err, and that on many doctrinal points Catholic and Protestant were in agreement. The leniency of James I and Charles I towards the recusants (except for a few months after the Gunpowder Plot, in 1605 and 1606) led to frustration, and during the Civil Wars and Interregnum a succession of revolutionary governments had been too busy suppressing or persecuting fellow Protestants to deal with the Catholics. Yet the Irish Rebellion of 1641, and the much-exaggerated massacres that attended it, had been another count against the Papists, who were also assumed by the common people to have ignited the Great Fire of London in 1666. Moreover, in the 1670s there was some reason to believe that Charles II had moved closer towards Catholicism than his father or his grandfather, and *their* conduct had been sufficiently unpopular in this respect. The fact that the Treaty of Dover contained secret clauses was widely suspected, and if the truth had been known at any time in the 1670s—that the King had undertaken to declare himself a Catholic and return the country to the Roman allegiance by force—his crown would almost certainly have been forfeit.

Moreover, there was James, Duke of York. Even in the early years of the Restoration, when he was a Protestant, James had been generally unpopular; he was regarded, in Shaftesbury's words, as "heady, violent and bloody, [a man] who easily believes the rashest and worst of counsels to be most sincere and hearty". After the fall of his father-in-law, Clarendon, in 1667 came the first proposals that Charles, failing legitimate issue, should take the Duke of Monmouth as his heir, and in 1670, when the House of Lords granted Lord Roos a divorce, Lord Ashley (later Earl of Shaftesbury) was one of those who proposed that the King should take the opportunity to rid himself of his barren wife and marry again. Meanwhile, rumours of James's conversion to Rome were widespread before 1672, when he ceased to take the Anglican Communion; in 1673 he resigned all his offices rather than take the new anti-Catholic test imposed by statute; and in 1676 he ceased to attend the Royal Chapel altogether. Thus England was faced with the prospect of a Catholic heir; and, though the Queen's childlessness could be taken for granted, the Duchess of York, at the age of nineteen, had already produced a daughter, Isabella, and a son, Charles, Duke of Cambridge, who had lived seven months. Conversely, after 1674 the Catholics had little more to hope for from Charles; the régime of militant Anglicanism at home and abroad established by Danby had culminated in 1677 in the marriage of James's eldest daughter and heiress Mary to William of Orange. The King was only three years older than his brother and might well outlive him, and though this was a balm to Protestant fears it also gave the Catholics a logical motive for assassination.

Add to all this the fact that the English public had the well-deserved reputation of being the most excitable and unstable in northern Europe and the credence generally given to the Plot is no longer so surprising. As for the educated classes, they were more than half convinced by the revelations contained in Coleman's letters and by the murder of Godfrey: two solid facts that ballasted the airiest of fictions. On 27 November Coleman was tried and found guilty of high treason, a verdict to which Oates's evidence contributed, and on 3 December he was executed, the first of fourteen victims. His death was an added incentive to belief, on the part of the populace, who could not believe that the Government had allowed an old and trusty servant of the Royal Family to be executed without due cause, and on the part of the governing classes, who must now share the responsibility for judicial murder if the Plot were admitted to be false.

But this does not explain the intensity and duration of the crisis that followed, a crisis that endangered not only Hereditary Succession but Divine Right, those twin pillars of the political order that had been so resoundingly confirmed in 1660 as to seem invulnerable.

A strong government could have surmounted the Popish Plot without serious embarrassment, but the Government of Charles II was far from being strong; in fact, even without the Plot it would almost certainly have been involved in a dangerous crisis in 1678 and 1679. It had never recovered from the humiliation of the years 1673-4, when the King had been forced to abandon the policy to which he stood committed: at home, religious toleration, and abroad, war against Holland. Four years of unremitting effort on Danby's part had done something to repair the damage, but not a great deal. Every Parliamentary session was still a hazardous adventure, every vote of taxation hung by a thread, while the reluctance of any section of Parliament to trust the King too far, and the divergence of purpose between him

and his chief Minister, paralysed his foreign policy. For
four years Charles had negotiated with Louis XIV and
with the United Provinces, and though in the spring of
1678 he apparently came down on the Dutch side, and
began assembling an army for war against France, he
still kept negotiations alive at Paris. But both Holland
and France were now heartily sick of the war, and
mistrustful of Charles. The peace negotiations at Nimwegen were speeded up and the war ended, quite
suddenly, in September 1678.

The peace of Nimwegen left Charles stranded. He had
a treaty of alliance with Holland, and another (secret)
with France. But neither of them was likely to be ratified.
He also had an army of 250,000, part in Flanders, part in
England, which he could not pay off without financial
assistance from Parliament. This alone would have made
for a restive session in October 1678. As it was, these
matters were overshadowed by the Plot, and here the
Government's record was fair. Charles had always been
sceptical, but Danby had shown admirable industry, and
it was directly due to him that Coleman's papers had
been seized before he could dispose of them. The Duke
of York was the Government's greatest handicap, but
even in this quarter they had their successes. When the
Commons, inevitably, produced a bill to exclude all
Catholics from Parliament (meaning, effectively, the
Upper House), the Lords sent it back with an amendment
excepting the Duke of York. There was a furious debate
in the Commons, but to the general surprise the amendment passed by two votes, on 20 November.

The decisive blow did not fall until 19 December,

when Ralph Montagu gave the Commons documentary proof that Danby had been engaged in secret negotiations for a treaty with France and the payment of a regular pension to Charles. The fact that this paragon of Protestant nationalism and Anglican respectability had been negotiating with the greatest Catholic despot in Europe shook the confidence of the very members of Parliament who had been his staunchest supporters. Four days later, his command of the Commons broken, he was impeached for high treason.

The situation was reminiscent of the impeachment of Strafford in 1640, and the charges were scarcely less serious: but the Lords, though they just lost twenty Catholic peers who had always been automatic supporters of the Government, were resolute. They refused to commit Danby, or even order him to withdraw; the Commons' spokesmen were not allowed to elaborate on the articles of impeachment, and he was given until 3 January to prepare a preliminary answer. Danby had every confidence in his ability to meet the charges made against him, and he was resentful when Charles suddenly prorogued Parliament for five weeks, from 30 December to 4 February. The public took this as a desperate attempt to save a guilty man, but at this stage the King was more anxious for his own reputation—for instance, he could never be sure that Montagu did not know of the secret Treaty of Dover and would not reveal it at a public trial. He was so rattled that on 24 Jan. 1679, he decided to take the tremendous risk of dissolving this eighteen-year-old Parliament and summoning another to meet on 6 March. Just before it met, he requested his brother to go abroad.

It had been decided that Danby would resign when Parliament met. He seems to have regarded this undertaking rather lightly; for instance, he spent several weeks trying to find a new Secretary of State who would strengthen his position in the Commons. But by the end of February it was clear that the elections had swept away his support in the lower House. The effects of these elections have been exaggerated, and the panicky estimates of contemporaries that the Court interest had been reduced to thirty are ridiculous. In May the Government could muster 128 supporters on the second reading of the Exclusion Bill; and there were many abstainers and absentees who would have turned up for the third reading. But Danby was the one man whom the courtiers could not defend, and Charles made a serious error when he allowed him to stay in office after the opening of the session. On 16 March his resignation was announced for Lady Day (25th): but by then it was too late. The news that Charles had granted him a full pardon, a marquessate, and a pension of £5,000 a year brought on his impeachment again, and Charles ordered him into hiding. The sudden removal of the King's chief Minister in mid-session completed the Government's disorder.

There is no reason to believe that the Lords would have handled Danby any more harshly than they had done at the end of the previous session. When Charles asked them to prepare a bill to banish Danby for life, his motive for ordering him into hiding became obvious; he hoped to do for him as he had done for Clarendon in 1667, and prevent a trial at whatever cost to his Minister's reputation. But Danby refused to flee abroad, and the

Commons this time would have nothing to do with a bill of banishment. After prolonged wrangling the Lords finally agreed to proceed against Danby by attainder unless he gave himself up by 16 April. He surrendered the evening before, and went to the Tower. The agitation at once subsided.

This four-week struggle to bring Danby to book, however, had diverted the attention and sapped the energies of the Opposition, and Charles had used the time well. On 21 April he appointed a new Privy Council of thirty which contained none of Danby's old henchmen; instead it contained a representative selection of the Opposition in both Houses: the Earl of Shaftesbury, Lord Russell, Lord Halifax, the Earl of Essex, Henry Powle, William Harbord and several more. Essex was appointed First Lord of the Treasury and Shaftesbury Lord President of the Council. (Charles I had contemplated a similar scheme in the spring of 1641, but in the end he was too scrupulous to attempt it.) A few days later he put forward a number of limitations on the powers of a Catholic monarch, especially on his powers of appointment, which were at once accepted by Essex and Halifax, on the assumption that Charles would never consent to the only alternative solution—James's exclusion from the succession.

This was enough to break the solidarity of the Opposition peers. Their leader, Shaftesbury, still favoured a compromise solution, such as the King's divorce: but the majority of his supporters in the Commons demanded James's exclusion from the succession. This, and perhaps jealousy of Essex and Halifax, induced Shaftesbury to support an Exclusion Bill which was brought into the Commons on 15 May—a step that was certainly premature, if not worse. The event confirmed his fears; the Bill passed its second reading by only 207 votes to 128, and the Opposition were in no hurry to bring on the third reading. They were still hesitating on 27 May, when Parliament was suddenly prorogued.

The worst of the crisis seemed over. Danby had been cleanly disposed of, and the King's skilful reconstruction of the Government had improved his position considerably. The rank-and-file of the Opposition no longer trusted their leaders. James was out of the way, and the support for exclusion was not overwhelmingly strong. The Bill would undoubtedly pass the Commons, but not by a large majority; and the House of Lords, which had shown itself so staunch in defence of the indefensible Danby, could be relied on to reject it or cripple it by amendment. Even the investigation of the Plot was losing momentum. Since the New Year, twelve men had been indicted, convicted, and executed on Oates's and Bedloe's evidence, including Whitbread, the head of the English Province of the Society of Jesus, and seven of his subordinates; but on 18 July Oates suffered a decisive check. At the trial of Sir George Wakeman, Lord Chief Justice Scroggs detected him in an obvious lie, summed up in the accused's favour and secured his acquittal. This was the first crack in the fabric of the Plot. Subsequently, the acquittal of the Earl of Castlemaine and Sir Thomas Gascoigne confirmed that judges and juries were no longer so willing to accept the testimony of informers.

But, at this promising stage, Charles took the disastrous step of dissolving Parliament and summoning another for October. His reluctance to take this step was manifest. On 3 July he came up to Hampton Court from Windsor to meet the Privy Council; and, on the insistence of Sunderland, Essex, and Halifax, he then raised the issue. He was at once opposed, not only by the Exclusionist councillors, Russell and Shaftesbury, but also by the Lord Privy Seal, Anglesey, and the Lord Chancellor, Finch, whose loyalty was never in doubt. At the end of a stormy meeting, the Ministers persuaded him that the degree of opposition his proposal had roused confirmed its necessity, and that he must affirm his decision. But at the next Council meeting, on 10 July, his attempt to forbid discussion was useless, and there was another altercation. Finch only consented to draw up the necessary proclamation under protest, and Russell said in a fury, "he was afraid the first vote of the next Parliament would be to declare such as gave this advice enemies of his Majesty and his kingdoms".

The first Exclusion Parliament met in March 1679, at a crisis in English history, when many still believed that the King's life was threatened by a Popish Plot and many more were appalled at the prospect of the succession of the Catholic heir-presumptive, the King's brother, James, Duke of York. This Parliament—the first new one for eighteen years—had clearly been summoned to take stock of this situation: but it had scarcely opened its legislative programme when it was prorogued, at the end of May. A bill to exclude the Duke of York from the succession had not even been put to a third reading in the

Commons. Parliament was due to re-assemble on 14 August: but on 11 July it was dissolved by proclamation. The news roused a public storm, which was intensified when James returned from exile at the end of August. The elections in August and September were held in an atmosphere of frenetic excitement, and for the first time on the issue of Exclusion; the result was an overwhelming defeat for the Government, and a House of Commons more hostile and unco-operative than before. So menacing was the prospect that Charles did not meet Parliament again until October 1680.

Why, then, was the first Exclusion Parliament dissolved? James, from Brussels, and Danby, from the Tower, both earnestly advised it: but it is unlikely that Charles hearkened to the advice of either. On the other hand, there were not many whose advice he *could* take. Danby had been autocratic and extremely capable, his assistants mere puppets; his sudden fall had left the King without advisers of courage and experience. The summons to the Privy Council of the leaders of the Parliamentary Opposition was an astute political move, but it had made the Council incapable of offering a united or considered opinion on matters of state. Charles's leading advisers were the Earl of Sunderland, who was reckless and inexperienced, Sir William Temple, who was timorous and pessimistic, and the Earl of Essex and Lord Halifax. The pressure for a dissolution came from Essex and Halifax, who had broken with their old leader, Shaftesbury, in April by accepting the King's alternative concessions instead of Exclusion. They were regarded with suspicion by the older courtiers, and by James, and treated as renegades by their old friends in Opposition. Their self-confidence had been undermined, and they snatched at any means of evading their present difficulties and responsibilities.

What arguments they used on the King‾are not clear; unless they harped on the possible danger from his illegitimate son, James, Duke of Monmouth. An attractive and pleasing young man, and a good soldier, Monmouth had had a few supporters willing to back his claims to the succession as early as 1668, at which time there were rumours that Charles had in fact been married to his mother, Lucy Walter. He had always been enormously popular with the common people, especially in London, and his uncle James was suspicious and jealous of him—so much so that before he left for Brussels in March 1679 he demanded that Charles solemnly and publicly declare that he had never married anyone but the Queen. In Parliament Monmouth's supporters were a tiny minority: but he was still Captain-General of the Army; and in June he was sent north to suppress the Covenanters' Rebellion in Scotland. His immediate success raised his popularity in the South to new heights, and the Ministers, aware of his growing involvement with Shaftesbury, feared that he would return to London in the role of conquering hero and put overwhelming pressure on his father, perhaps even use military force, to ensure an early re-assembly of Parliament.

Charles himself cannot have taken this seriously, though there was always a powerful bond of affection between him and his son. Moreover, though many historians have taken it for granted that the aim of Shaftesbury and the majority of the Exclusionists was to place Monmouth on the throne, there is little evidence for this, and a great deal against it. As one modern historian puts it, "Very few of the Whig section of the 'political nation' ever countenanced or committed themselves to his claims", and another remarks, "The whole Exclusion movement was against the Duke of York, and not for the Duke of Monmouth". The principle of legitimate succession was woven into the entire fabric of English law and society; and no Parliament consisting mainly of landowners or heirs to land can have been expected to overthrow it. The first Exclusion Bill laid it down that the Crown should pass as though James were legally dead; should pass, that is, to his eldest daughter, Mary; and the only voices raised against this were those of anonymous pamphleteers not sanctioned by the Parliamentary leaders. Until November 1680 at the earliest, Shaftesbury cultivated Monmouth because of his personal influence over the King; and, when he could, he cultivated Charles's mistress, the Duchess of Portsmouth, for the same reason.

But from the dissolution of the first Exclusion Parliament the crisis entered upon a new and much more acute stage. After Wakeman's acquittal, the Plot was relegated to the background, giving new emphasis to the other great issue before the public: James's fitness for the kingship. James himself underlined this when he suddenly returned from exile at the end of August, on the news of the King's serious illness. It has too often been assumed that James's influence was merely negative, and always disastrous: but this is a false assumption. Events since March had shown that many of the governing classes were opposed to Exclusion: but, with Danby gone, they were leaderless, incoherent, and drifting. James gave them leadership. He forced Charles to bar from Court all those whose allegiance was doubtful; he made him send Monmouth into exile; and he made him prorogue the new Parliament until the following January without even meeting it. He himself retired to Edinburgh in November, where he had the backing of the powerful and efficient Scots army.

The Exclusionists' reply was feeble. Essex resigned from the Treasury: but he was replaced by Lawrence Hyde, a man devoted to James's interests. Essex and Halifax, who had been the chief element of instability in the ministry, virtually retired from public life for the next six months. Monmouth returned from abroad in November, without permission, and was at once dismissed all his offices. He had now dropped the bend sinister from his arms; and his supporters were busy with rumours of the Black Box that was supposed to contain his mother's marriage certificate. *An Appeal from the Country to the City* put him forward as a candidate for the throne, on the cynical argument that his defective title would make him of necessity an easy-going ruler: but his very popularity with the City mobs was enough to prejudice his case with the upper classes.

Shaftesbury finally resorted to a campaign of mass petitioning for an early meeting of Parliament: but Charles merely issued a proclamation forbidding tumultuous and riotous petitioning, and announced that he would not meet Parliament until November 1680. Shaftesbury's position was now so weak, in December 1679, that even this was not enough to make him resign; and he and his followers did not leave the Council until a month later, when Charles announced that he was recalling his brother from Scotland.

James's return in February 1680 further stiffened the supporters of the Crown. Doubts about his suitability for the throne were weakening; the Plot, with Roman Catholicism, was no longer a serious political issue. The Church had rallied to the cause of Divine Right and Hereditary Succession; and the lay Anglicans, too, led by James's brother-in-law, Lawrence Hyde, regarded him as bulwark against the spread of Protestant Dissent. The Exclusionist petitions were answered by counter-petitions "abhorring" this practice, and the clumsy names "petitioners" and "abhorrers" were soon abandoned in favour of "Whigs" and "Tories". A year before James's cause seemed likely to pass by default; it was now revealed that he had a powerful body of support in the nation at large. Trading on this, the Government, in the spring of 1680, undertook a complete purge of the lists of magistrates and deputy-lieutenants throughout the country, removing all those whose loyalty was doubtful. This undermined the morale of the rank-and-file Exclusionists; and their leaders were drifting. The petitioning campaign had failed; Shaftesbury had quarrelled with many of his closest associates, like Ralph Montagu; and others had even gone abroad. By November it looked as though Exclusion would be dead.

The reasons for the Whig revival that followed, in the

second half of 1680, are still not fully understood; and some would even argue that it was not a genuine revival but a mere flash in the pan; an argument supported by the Whigs' ignominious collapse in 1681. The revival began at the end of June, when Shaftesbury had the temerity to indict James as a recusant before the Middlesex Grand Jury, sitting in Westminster Hall. This act of defiance encouraged the Whigs of the City of London so much that, the following month, the Government failed in a well-publicised attempt to seize control of the City at the elections to the Common Council—a coup that it had every expectation of bringing off. Henceforward, it was the instability of the capital that obliged Charles to meet Parliament, as an alternative to an insurrection. His other motive for summoning Parliament was to test its support for an anti-French foreign policy. If Parliament would not support this policy, based on treaties with Holland, Spain, and the Empire, then it would support no foreign policy at all, and it could be discounted in this extremely important sphere of operations.

When this Parliament met, in October 1680, it was much more hostile to the Crown, and more strongly in favour of Exclusion, than its predecessor. Some of this must be attributed to the elections thirteen months before. But many moderate men had also been swung over towards extremism by Charles's purge of local government, the most comprehensive yet attempted, and by his manœuvres to avoid meeting Parliament, which were reminiscent of Charles I and the Duke of Buckingham at their worst. The premature dissolution of the previous Parliament, a Parliament with an obvious mandate, was particularly deeply resented; and, as Russell had foretold, the second Exclusion Parliament spent some time trying to apportion the blame for this decision and bring the offenders to book. Finally, James's belligerence, and the great measure of support he obviously enjoyed, at Whitehall and in the country, alarmed many who had voted against his Exclusion in the previous Parliament; and Charles's serious illness in the autumn of 1679, followed by a slight relapse the following spring, was an uncomfortable reminder of his mortality. Monmouth had made a campaigning tour of the West Country just before Parliament met; and, early in November, Russell dared to produce an Exclusion Bill which had no safeguards for the legitimate succession. The Tories were strong enough to remedy this at once: but they did not feel strong enough to bring the bill itself to a division, and it passed its third reading on 11 November.

London was in an uproar; and it was generally believed that Shaftesbury had organised his lower-class followers for a revolt if the bill did not pass the Lords. Deputations from the City waited on the King to inform him of this: but he was unmoved. He had sent his brother back to Edinburgh the day before Parliament met: but he had announced then that he would in no circumstances accept Exclusion; and in this he was firm, despite the defection of leading ministers like Sunderland and Godolphin. His views were again made plain in a Message to the Commons on 9 November, and re-inforced by personal messages to individual peers of influence. When the bill appeared in the Lords on

15 November, he came down to the Chamber in person and sat through the debate.

This debate has often been represented as an oratorical triumph for Lord Halifax. Perhaps it was: the evidence is too scanty to tell: but oratory scarcely affected the result. It was unthinkable that the House of Lords should defy the King's express wishes and vote for the bill; and since the beginning of the crisis Shaftesbury had never been able to muster more than twenty supporters among his peers. This total was swelled to thirty now by the defection of several Government spokesmen: but the majority against was sixty-three. Only one thing might have induced the Lords to give way; and that was the threat of immediate civil war. But if they passed the bill they would not avert this threat. James, established in Scotland, sure of support from Ireland, and perhaps also from France, had made it uncompromisingly clear that he would not accept Exclusion without putting the issue to the arbitration of the sword; and in such an encounter he would have plenty of support in England, too. Halifax gave this argument great prominence in the debate on the Exclusion Bill, when he warned the Lords that there was nothing to prevent James detaching Scotland and Ireland from England. The Earl of Yarmouth asserted, in the same debate: "[There is] no law strong enough to fence out an indisputable title; it will entail a war to posterity, dismember[ing] and lessening the bounds of this Empire".

The King's gamble came off. London did not rise in revolt; and the provinces had never seemed likely to. The Opposition were unable to use their power in the

Commons to any constructive end; and, by declining to prorogue them, Charles gave them no chance to introduce another Exclusion Bill. Bolder spirits might have impeached James—it was a similar threat to the Queen that had stampeded Charles I in 1642—but Charles II was a much tougher, more flexible man than his father; and such an impeachment could have been held up indefinitely in the Lords. (Danby had been impeached eighteen months before: but his trial had not yet started.) Still, the Whigs' activities in Parliament in November and December 1680 were singularly pointless and non-constructive: they had the disadvantage of a one-plank platform. In desperation, Shaftesbury was being driven to lend Monmouth firmer and more decisive support: but the political wisdom of this was dubious. By January 1681, Charles was in sight of success, though few recognised it. He dissolved Parliament, dismissed all his servants who had voted for Exclusion, and summoned another Parliament to meet at Oxford in March. He went to Oxford with a full escort of Guards; for he calculated that only by armed revolt could the Whigs hope to succeed. The elections were conducted in the usual lather of excitement: but the results are difficult to assess, as this Parliament sat only for a week.

The tide had now turned. Perhaps it had turned the previous spring; certainly it had turned in November, when the Lords threw out the Exclusion Bill. Charles's manipulations of Parliament, his prorogations, dissolutions, and now this change of venue, did not inspire confidence. But the Whigs were not putting forward measures designed to halt this abuse—an amended

Triennial Act, for instance. They insisted that any such laws would be pointless if a Catholic monarch succeeded to the throne, and that Exclusion therefore must come first, second and last. This was all very well: but, by the end of 1680, the Whig leaders had been made to appear insanely obstinate and provocative in pushing the one measure that was absolutely certain to cause civil war, now or on Charles's death, and refusing the King's conciliatory offers, which in March 1681 even extended to a regency after his death, administered by the Princess Mary or her husband.

The Exclusion movement was not provoked merely by the Popish Plot; after all, James's unsuitability for the throne had been a political issue as long as ten years before. It expressed the frustration and anger of the Parliamentary classes, or large sections of them, with the King's foreign policy since his restoration, and his domestic policy since 1672. It drew its strength from a group of perfectly ordinary gentry, most of them loyal Anglicans, who were deeply hostile to Popery, and whose confidence and stability had been badly shaken by the betrayal of Danby's secret foreign policy. Their fears on this issue had now been allayed—or at least, they now saw that the price to pay for calming them might be too high. Their panic over the Popish Plot had died down. The rise in the fortunes of the illegitimate candidate, Monmouth, and the open support given by many Opposition leaders to Protestant Dissent, gave them pause; and the firm stand taken by the Anglican Church, to which most of them belonged, could not help but have its effect. Only a trifling minority wanted a bastard to

ascend the English throne, and an even smaller minority
wanted civil war—except as a last resort, to fend off a
Popish despotism which was no longer so threatening
as it had been; and their powerlessness to affect the
elections of January and February 1681 probably
frightened them more than anything else. The increasing
influence of the unfranchised mobs on Parliamentary
elections was one of the features of this crisis; and it
threatened the political influence of many landowners.
Moreover, some of the Whig leaders were known to be
favourable to reforms of the franchise and the representation along the lines taken by Cromwell's advisers in
1654—the disenfranchisement of corrupt boroughs and
an increase in county seats so as to increase the power of
the small freeholder at the expense of his landlord. If a
triumphant Parliament forced Exclusion on the King, this
was the sort of legislative programme that would follow.

It is not difficult to see why, when Charles abruptly
dissolved the Oxford Parliament, the Exclusion movement collapsed. The aristocratic leaders were ready to go
on; so were the small fringe of republicans and adven-
turers whom the movement had attracted: but the great
mass of smaller men, who had voted for Exclusion in the
Commons, merely dwindled away. The King left Oxford
in a hurry; but his Parliament was not far behind.
"Round them," writes David Ogg, "were tennis courts
and college gardens on which the Commons might have
reunited themselves by an oath more solemn than any
which they had yet sworn: but they dispersed; some to
London, others to the country, and many to the horse
races at Burford."

SELECT BIBLIOGRAPHY

ASHLEY, M. *The Glorious Revolution of 1688*. London (Hodder & Stoughton) 1966. The latest account.

AYLMER, G. E. *The King's Servants 1625-1642*. London (Routledge) 1961. The court and the Civil Service.

BARNES, T. G. *Somerset 1625-1640*. Oxford (University Press) 1961. Government and outlook of a county.

BAXTER, S. B. *William III*. London (Longmans) 1966. The best life of "Dutch William".

BELOFF, M. *Public Order and Popular Disturbances 1660-1714*. Oxford (University Press) 1938.

BINDOFF, S. T. *Ket's Rebellion*. London (Historical Association) 1949. A useful pamphlet.

CHAPMAN, H. *The Last Tudor King*. London (Cape) 1958.

— *Lady Jane Grey*. London (Cape) 1962. Two popular biographies.

Crisis in Europe 1560-1660, ed. T. Aston. London (Routledge) 1965. Essays on "the general crisis".

DAVIES, G. *The Restoration of Charles II*. San Marino, Calif. (Huntingdon Library) 1956. The fullest account.

DICKENS, A. G. *The English Reformation*. London (Batsford) 1962. Brilliant.

Elizabethan Government and Society, eds. S. T. Bindoff *et al.* London (Athlone Press) 1961. See especially Hurstfield, J., "The Succession Struggle in late Elizabethan England".

ELTON, G. R. *England under the Tudors*. London (Methuen) 1955.

— *Star Chamber Stories*. London (Methuen) 1958.

— *The Tudor Constitution*. Cambridge (University Press) 1960. Elton is always thorough and incisive.

HARRISON, G. B. *Robert Devereux, Earl of Essex*. London (Cassell) 1937. Rather slight.

HILL, C. *The Century of Revolution 1603-1714*. Edinburgh (Nelson) 1961. Strong on analysis.

Historical Essays 1600-1750, eds. H. E. Bell and R. L. Ollard. London (Black) 1963. See especially H. R. Trevor-Roper on "Scotland and the Great Rebellion".

HEXTER, J. H. *Reappraisals in History*. London (Longmans) 1961. Provocative essays.

HURSTFIELD, J. *Elizabeth I and the Unity of England*. London (English Universities Press) 1961. Brief but comprehensive.

JONES, J. R. *The First Whigs 1678-83*. Oxford (University Press) 1961. The fullest account of the Exclusion Crisis.

KENYON, J. P. *The Stuarts*. London (Batsford) 1958. Pungent.

— *The Stuart Constitution 1603-88*. Cambridge (University Press) 1966.

LEVINE, M. *The Early Elizabethan Succession Question*. Stanford, Calif. (University Press) 1966. Very full.

LOADES, D. M. *Two Tudor Conspiracies*. Cambridge (University Press) 1965. Wyatt's and Dudley's risings.

NEALE, J. E. *Essays in Elizabethan History*. London (Cape) 1958.

NOBBS, D. *England and Scotland 1558-1707*. London (Hutchinson) 1953.

PARMITER, G. de C. *The King's Great Matter*. London (Longmans) 1967. Henry VIII's "divorce".

PEARL, V. *London and the Outbreak of the Puritan Revolution*. Oxford (University Press) 1961.

PLUMB, J. H. *Political Stability in England 1675-1725*. London (Macmillan) 1967. Stimulating lectures.

PRESCOTT, H. M. F. *Mary Tudor*. London (Eyre & Spottiswoode) 1952. The best life.

RILEY, P. W. J. *The English Ministers and Scotland 1707-21*. London (Athlone Press) 1964.

ROOTS, I. *The Great Rebellion 1642-60*. London (Batsford) 1966. Narrative with emphasis on 1650s.

SACHSE, W. L. "The Mob and the Revolution of 1688" in *Journal of British Studies*, IV (1964).

STONE, L. *The Crisis of the Aristocracy 1558-1641*. Oxford (University Press) 1965 ; abridged ed. 1967. Important.

— *Social Change and Revolution in England 1540-1640*. London (Longmans) 1965. Extracts from contemporaries and recent historians.

SUPPLE, B. *Commercial Crisis and Change 1600-1642*. Cambridge (University Press) 1959. Valuable on social policy.

TURNER, F. C. *James II*. London (Eyre & Spottiswoode) 1952. The best life.

WEDGWOOD, C. V. *The Great Rebellion*: I. *The King's Peace 1637-41*. London (Collins) 1955; II. *The King's War 1641-47*. London (Collins) 1958. Very full narrative.

WERNHAM, R. B. *Before the Armada*. London (Cape) 1966. Tudor foreign policy.

WHITE, H. *Social Criticism in Popular Religious Literature of the Sixteenth Century*. New York (Macmillan) 1944.

WITCOMBE, D. T. *Charles II and the Cavalier House of Commons 1663-74*. Manchester (University Press) 1966.

WOOLRYCH, A. H. "The Good Old Cause and the Fall of the Protectorate", in *Cambridge Historical Journal*, XIII (1957).